NEW & SELECTED POEMS
1994-2002

ACKNOWLEDGEMENTS

With grateful acknowledgement to Goose Lane Editions for poems from *Resisting the Anomie* and Ohio University Press for poems from *Midland*.

KWAME DAWES

NEW & SELECTED POEMS
1994-2002

PEEPAL TREE

First published in Great Britain in 2003
Peepal Tree Press Ltd
17 King's Avenue
Leeds LS6 1QS
England

ISBN 1 900715 70 8

CONTENTS

from *Requiem*–1996

from *Shook Foil*–1997

Some of my worst wounds
have healed into poems

Lorna Goodison

poems from

RESISTING THE ANOMIE

WHAT DID YOU SAY?

for Kofi Awoonor

Did you speak to him
when he came to you
drawn by the smell of rum
thick in the muggy night
with the odd star darting?

Did his arch of arm
skyward head and muttering lips
translate themselves and summon you
to this libation of rum and water?

Uncle Kofi wrapped his cloth around him and walked barefoot
through the grass with peace on his face. You were brother to him,
he said, as he remembered as I did your words, *J. Christ Esquire?*
Never met the fellow, but the ancestors walk beneath this earth.

They drank rum all night
speaking of you.

At dawn they rose
gathered their cloth
consoled Mama
and departed

three princes of Africa
come to pay homage
to a comrade.

AFTER 'ACCEPTANCE'

Then I read the monumental legend of her love
And grasp her wrinkled hands
    'Acceptance' by Neville Dawes

i

You were a child there
from two
to introverted ten
crafting your dreams
from tattered books
teacher Dawes crammed
onto his shelves.
Your brother was a knight
and your sisters princesses
and you wrote verse
because you longed for friends.

Curled in the cool underpart
of the creaking house on the hill
you battled chickens for space to sketch
the worlds in your head.

ii

We drove there together once,
you, proud of recollections stirred,
endeared each sharp bend in the road
with names like Breadfruit Curve,
Star Apple Corner and Tamarind Arch.
Your laughter was nervous nearing the house,
the child in you drumming a rhythm
on the sweat-slick steering wheel.

On the slack porch you pointed
through breadfruit leaves
to the fading line of sea and sky
where Cuba wavered
in the midday haze.

From there as child
you learnt of otherness, worlds beyond the house
afloat in a sea of green.
From there your home became
a point from which to leap.

iii

I walk the overgrown paths
where fired with Arthurian legends
you galloped, mad-child
on a wild irreverent steed
dizzy in the patchwork
of sunlight through branches.

The thought of you as child
is real as the trees towering.
And staring upwards
I trace your steps
avoiding the trunks
by the pattern of leaves
in the sky.
The child overwhelms
my straight-back logic
and suddenly I am sprinting
beating hoofbeats against my chest
light blazing green on my face
my shouts echoed in the tree trunks.

On the barbecue
dry brown pimento beans roast,
the ancient chair she sat in
is there where a rotting orange tree
leans and sheds brittle leaves.
The chair is light and fading
sucked dry by sun and salt wind.

I can see her bandannaed there
sharp calico against the hill's grey
her wrinkled hands outstretched, trembling
her eyes glowing.

v

Maybe your ghosts hover above the house at nights,
but I came at daytime, so I am not sure, but teachers,
you taught me much in the lesson of your silent ways.

While there, I smell ink and the dust I sneezed was chalk dust.
Your world was a noble one, the cloud of holy witnesses
who sought new worlds to replace the chain link silences.

Daily Bible verses etched on your brow missionary zeal
and gave strength to your upright eyes. Now you hover above
this house that crumbles where the wood ticks termites.

Maybe, grand ones, your ghosts linger above the house,
meeting there, then together swoop down, one wind
lifting a tattered sheet's edge – now animated, now brilliant O

cooling with a breath the sheen of toil on some weary back,
shifting breadfruit leaves to a rustling as eyes turn upward
smiling at the cool, not at you, not knowing that ghosts are wind.

You return morose, having done your part of touching the
     living before dawn
and getting little thanks for it. You return to your tombs in
     which you were sheltered
from the swelter of sun and the tramping of my feet now in
     the grey and green

.

vi

I praise the dream of Sturge Town
and the silent homecoming it was

I praise the songs of the ghosts
sealed in my mind's chysalis.

I praise the constant leaves
spinning in the pure air

I praise the hands that birthed you
worn as they were

for they glowed
stained red with first blood

spilled into this navel-string soil
where for years

the ancient red-barked trees
have stood.

I praise these things
freed by her wrinkled hands.

17

CHIEF

For John Ruganda

I have, since that moment
staring into the red tenderness of your open head
on the stainless steel tray
before we bundled you like a mummy
and laid you on old *Gleaners* in the back
of the station wagon,

I have, since that moment,
adopted fathers repeatedly,
with pathological consistency
searching for that wizened mentor
to talk adult verse with.

And in this fragile city of elms
my father is statuesque Ugandan
a king from a land of tall-headed royalty,
peering through thick lenses,
tricks in his eyes –
ageless carving in ebony
regal in the half-light of the club
the head straight and chiselled –
through the mist of rum and water.

My father calls me to a caucus
welcoming me like an uninitiated chief
and we talk, wiping away the mystery,
scratching images into the sand
vulnerable whisperings
that understand betrayal
and shun it.

He slants towards the plane one winter night
and the image of your body wrapped in the white linen
assails my mind sudden and intense.
I do not watch the plane lift and vanish.
The road is wet and slick as we drive home.
I am crying,

Please God don't let this airplane crash.
Please God don't let this airplane crash.
Please God don't let this airplane crash.

Intoning like a child staring into the sky
blessing each plane that thunders overhead
for caution's sake in case it is you, father,
returning from journeyings into the mysterious worlds
far from this dry pampas of bush and concrete.

THE DAY YOU PLAYED THE PIANO

We entered the hall.
Black wood tiles glowed.
The hollow sound of feet
did not startle you
drowned in the tinkle of the piano
jazz bopping with right-hand trills,
feet tap-tapping on the squeaking brass pedals.

We gathered round
watching those soft fingers
spread and tighten
on the white and black
obeying the fugue
in your head.

We never knew.

Yet we should have
thinking back to the days
gathered around the reel-to-reel
sucked in by Lady Day's
bitter-fruit-blues
and watching you walk-dance
half-stepping, half-jiving
to the drone and wail
of the piano turns.

We should have known
from your blue silences
as if reaching
for some poem eluding you,
we should have guessed it was a tune
trying to wake fingers
to dance on supple keys.

PROPHECY

The voice was in my heart.
It came in there and spoke.
From the hills it was clear.
Exile from the cragged dustiness
of the scarred road winding up
that skyline hill which is a line
of twisting lights at night.

I left because God told me to.
At first I was able to say this casually,
for it was the truth, it is the truth.
Now, I lie. I talk about opportunity,
about the beauty of a foreign degree.
I lie.

Skyline is still there with grey-green scraggly bush,
rocky hillside like a desert landscape, not flat,
and the voice of the Lord is caught in the bramble
and sometimes on the hillside bushes burn.

ON LEAVING HOME

I leave behind the dark hillside
enveloped with the mist
rushing down from the mountains
in sudden chilly gusts

I leave behind the clapping
the stomping of feet
the word in season
the home in their smiles

I leave behind the boards
creaking with our uncertain attempts
to make flesh of the words on the page
brought forth by the miracle of prophecy

I leave behind the voices
the music in the uneasy vans
playing roulette with the traffic lights
and the chaos of pedestrians

I repeat the ritual of departure
as one would rehearse lines
remembering details
by the position of the head or hand,

the climate, the angle of the sun
on the window, the noise
of mornings. I test them
these small icons to see

if maybe I might miss them.
For days I carry out
this ritual of leaving until
I am sure I have mastered it.

HISTORY LESSON AT EIGHT A.M.

History class at eight a.m.
Who discover Jamaica, class?
Christopher Columbus
Tell me when?
Fourteen ninety-two
And where?

Discovery Bay
Discovery Bay

Twisting through Mount Diablo
Where Juan de Bolas was hiding
Musket, fife and powder
Guerilla, revolutionary
I am travelling to Discovery Bay
Travelling to Discovery Bay

How many ships?
Three ship
What them name?
Nina
One
Pinta
Two
Santa Maria
Tell me where?

Discovery Bay
Discovery Bay

Twisting through Fern Gully
Arawak blood was shed here
Crack their brains with musket shot

History is buried here
I am travelling to Discovery Bay
travelling to Discovery Bay

Who lived here first?
Arawak and Carib
What were the Arawak?
Peaceful flat-head people
What were the Caribs?
Cannibals
Cannibals?
Yes, cannibals!
Now tell me where?

Discovery Bay
Discovery Bay

Rush past St. Ann's Bay
Marcus was preaching from the altar
See the slave auction inna Falmouth
Cane field wild with fire
I am travelling to Discovery Bay
Travelling to Discovery Bay

You teach me all kind of madness
From Hawkins to Drake to Pizarro
From Cortez to Penn to Venables
At eight a.m. each blessed day
No wonder I can't find Discovery Bay
Was looking for the gold

And all I see is blood
All I see is blood
All I see is blood

THELMA'S PRECIOUS CARGO

She was bringing fried fish, festival,
banana, dumpling, roast corn,
sweet sugar cane, nicely peel and cool
when the plastic-gloved customs officer
squinge up him nose like him smelling his upper lip
decide to break every fruit
gut open the fish, spilling all that white flesh
and sweet fried tomato all over the counter.

Say him was searching for drugs
searching for disease
from this great-grandmother with
centuries springing in her eyes
who come just to catch a sight
of the children she never met
and who might grow up without
the grounding of stories she been
carrying all these years.

But Thelma never panic before
no child, she simply gather the ruins
and then spread her bandanna –
flaming red with yellow light –
on the blue stale carpet in a corner
and she place every injured offering
on the shimmering surface.

Thelma light a red candle and draw a circle
round the feast like a prayer
and then she invite the people them
who line up to face the plastic-glove man
to come sit with she and her grandson
who smiling like he can't stop all this time

and eat a good sunrise meal
no fuss, just this laughing in her eyes.

And them drink off all the sweetsop juice
lace with a little Appleton fire
and them eat that food like communion
and when them was finished
Thelma say a prayer and whisper
a little forgiveness to the bwoy with the gloves.

And them calmly wobble through the customs
clean as a priest before service
with all the drugs and disease
swimming and singing in them belly
walking like that into the sweet Canadian air
warm as ever and ready.

And Thelma tell the story again and again
and end it with the last sweet lines

Child, them shoulda follow we to the toilet
the day, for some of them seed find soil
and see the tree them there still.
Africa people been carrying them possessions in them shit
forever. Precious cargo, child, precious cargo.

And man we couldn't stop laugh

poems from

PROGENY OF AIR

ON BEING UNCKA'S BROTHER

For Kojo

My big brother did not protect me.
He watched his friends stand me up
against the huge ficus tree by the gate

and command me to sing while rubbing my belly.
I sang 'In heaven there is no beer', and
belched for them. They laughed and slapped

my grinning brother on the back.
We did not speak for days.
It was years later that I understood

the burden of his shame,
watching me with his nose and eyes
forehead greasy in the sun

looking like a sorry version
of Uncka the fighter, my brother.
Maybe they expected me to growl,

struggle, throw some punches
like a true little 'Uncka Uncka Kill Kill'
Africa boy would; but I only stood there

rubbed my belly and sang,
missing the point of having
a celebrated fighter for a big brother.

EXCURSION TO PORT ROYAL

> i am inside of
> history
> its
> hungrier than i
> thot.
>
> *Ishmael Reed*

In the giddy house   the wind riots on the beach
where we have had a lunch of flat moist sandwiches cooked
by the steaming bus engine   now alone
abandoned by the other boys   I stare across the roll of sea
there is no sign of the passing of time

no evidence of the decades of progress
only the scraggly grass   the Institute of Jamaica
tourist information plaque screwed tight
into the armoury wall   here is the possibility of journey
from the quarterdeck I claim all I survey

on Admiral Nelson's quarterdeck the sea sand is black
shells glint white in the tick of waves
the water is moving   the horizon shifts   the morning's clean edge
smudges into stark sheets of white light   a thin line of cloud
moves   the wind toying with its tail.

canon crusted with centuries of rust   black sea sand   dirt points
Admiral Nelson surveys the royal port from his quarterdeck
goblet of gold rum swishing in his unsteady hands   the bitch is singing
from the wooden whorehouse a blue yorkshire shanty
        her tongue
is heavy on the vowels   his dick is erect

here was Napoleon's nemesis too   long haired bitch with a royal name
teasing the rum to flame in the sweet roast fish air   singing Josephines
their tongues dancing   in the voice you smell their sex
Nelson searches the horizon for a ship's sail needling its way
across the fabric of green silk looking for war

the shore crunches   laps   folds   unfolds   ticks   gravels
its undertow back out to the seaweed bed   the last of the rum
warms sweetly in his pit   the voice sirens across the quad
and making his giddy way past the armoury   combustible
as this itch in his pants   Nelson prays for the empire

NEWCOMER

the first ejaculation —
a cliff beyond which lies
hell-fire, brimstone,

insanity, blue balls
hair in the palm, death
in this pain like laughter

as this press of energy
fights for its uncharted
irrevocable explosion

i smile at the seed
brimful of light
spilled in this security

of trees under the all-
seeing eye of a
three o'clock sky

behind my old
primary school
the relief lies

in the sweetness
of the coming
and afterwards

the ability to still find
all body parts
intact, in place

OFF THE MARK

Here panting in the rat-smelling dark
is my squandered innocence;
spilt seed on the urine-smelling mattress

where this girlchild, casual as love,
sleeps in fits and starts, wrestling her
nightmares, her mouth open and dripping.

Waking, she declares again her love for me
clasping my startled body hard
against her tremble, and kisses

me a mouthful of sour wine, her tongue
clumsy against my teeth. I want
to run away with my softening member now drowned

by the sperm swimming in the condom.
While I weep confession to my God,
still shaking from the revelation of the ejaculate's riotous exit,

I spy her smiling in the half-light, tossing
kisses across the room, her nipples dark
against the yellow transparent nightie.

She is confident as a betrothed princess
impatient for the song and feasting of the ceremony.
What I feel is not love, it is that tight throat

of sorrow on a dark rainy day, that
bigness of tears ready to flow
uncontrollable as a suppressed giggle;

it is the guilt of sin, burden of my youth
here in this room where I have broken
my proverbial duck, gotten off the mark, scored.

ALADO SEANADRA

Something like forty runs to pile up in fifteen overs
with the sun round like power over the compound.
I prayed like hell out there on the boundary

far from the scorers talking Test cricket as if this game
was another day in the sun. I prayed like hell.
I had made something like twenty – out to a stupid short ball

which should have been dispatched to mid-wicket
with ease. But too greedy, I got a top edge,
and was caught looking naked as a fool in the blazing

midmorning. Now, like a mockery, the bowling was soup
but the boys still struggling to put one single before a next.
So I prayed like hell out there on the boundary, trying to will

a flaming red four my way. Still, I should have known,
after all, God's dilemma: We playing a Catholic team
that always prayed before each game. And where their chapel

was a shrine, ours, well sometimes goats get away
inside there; and once we did a play right there using the altar
as a stage. So I tried making deals with the Almighty,

taking out a next mortgage on my soul; asking him to
strengthen the loins of Washy who looking alone in the wilderness
out there in the blaze, bedlamized by the googly

turning on the rough patch outside off-stump.
Washy went playing at air, and the wickets kept falling
until it was Alado, flamboyant with his windmill stretch action,

his fancy afro and smile, strutting out to the wicket
still dizzy with the success of his bowling that morning.
And Alado take his guard loud, loud to the umpire:

'Middle and leg, please.' Lean back till his spine crack.
Alado, slow like sugar, put on the tips, prolonging the agony.
Now, Alado surveying the field, from boundary to

boundary as if somebody was about to move a stone,
and the boys start to wonder if this was some
secret weapon, some special plan to win the match

in a trickifying way. I fantasised a miracle
in that moment, but I blame the sun for that.
And then the boy take his stance. Classic poise, bat tapping,

looking like a test class stroke-player, toes shuffling,
waiting for the pace bowler sprinting stallion along the worn
dry grass. Up to the wicket, he bowls, good length ball,

dead on mid and off. Alado shift the front foot forward,
sheer poise and style, head down according to the Boycott book,
elbow up, and unleash a full cover drive,

bat like flying fish catching the sun. And even when we heard
the clunk of the stumps, and see the bails take off,
we all still searching the extra cover boundary

to see the ball slap the boards. Alado Test stay posed off
like that for Lord knows how long. Big smile in his eyes
staring at the ball he must have hit in his dreams.

The umpire signal end of play with the gathering of the bails
and the pulling of the stumps. My soul was saved that day,
the year we never made the finals.

PERCH IN FLIGHT

We called her Perch
for her fish-shocked eyes

and because the word
had a sound of sex to it.

It stuck.

She was not the type
boys would will their

wet dreams around;
instead, she slipped in

when we least expected it
and tormented our dreams.

This was because Perch
and her sexuality

were not fiction
born out of our wild

imaginings.

Perch had been caught
spread and supine

on the woodwork table
cradling the woodwork

teacher between her thighs.
There were witnesses.

Boys are rarely cultivated
to be sensitive to women

and their bigness of
imagination and their

strength, so we teased
Perch when she least

needed it.

'Inna de woodwork room
Perch, Perch,

Inna de woodwork room.'
Quite simply,

we drove her mad.
We thought it funny

the way she rambled on
on the Prize Giving podium

her speech crumbling
into complete nonsense

until the spittle dried
at the corners of her mouth.

We snickered when
three burly teachers

from the P.E. department
dragged her off the podium

from under the shade
of the bottle green

mango leaves.

I laughed too.
Then there was the day I almost

walked into her in the city
and found our eyes met level

and hers softened with
recognition and smiled

sadly, like an old friend:
'As you see me here,

Dawes, still not married
yet, but I am trying.

They say you have to keep
trying. So, I am trying, nuh.'

This Perch,

this fish swimming
hard against the current

in her revival red
bandanna and dusty

feet in the schoolyard.
Maybe I loved her then

and in my dreams
I saw her with her lab-coat

flying, her test tubes
whistling melodies

through the play
of the blue wind.

THE ENGLISH ROOM

For Mr. Bobsemple

The desk is still broken, the floorboards
more rotted, the smell of circumspect rats
whose faces peek out only after the boys have left

lingers still. This was the old English room
where we parried Shakespearean quotes
and found magic in being infant poets.

Hopkins' sprung verse, uncaged passion
in praise of God and colour, was our appropriated
tutor. This quest for meaning and discovery

was like conquest, stabbing flag into willing sand;
it was hard to see the poetry for the notes,
rioting debates in shades of blue and snubbed

pencil, scribbled paths of our journeys on the pages'
edge. We loved his story of inconsequence while cloistered
in the belly of Christ's heart, walls around the leap

of verse into the fertile souls of parishioners
who heard his sermons ignorant of the secret box
of scribbled verse buried like possession in his cell.

This freedom to write the hidden; performing
for the starved eye of our imaginations,
made us dare to write our fragile poems;

not of poplars, not of the evergreen of Oxford lawns
not of Steven the farrier and his muddy boots,
but of the guinep tree unruly over the thirsty

yellow scraggly school grounds, and Racecourse
with his wheelbarrow and tragic machete with
a poem of passionate crimes in its blade's thin edge.

To construct passion sweet as a urine-smelling toilet,
a first ejaculation under sky and cocooning
mango groves; to find season in sudden storm

and sun. Here we saw colour in words,
numb, clumsy tongues curling around new
language and finding silence where the words

were not yet made. Where are they now, these
my fellow poets? Where gone? Do they ever,
shuffling paper and memos in air-conditioned

conformity, walls stuccoed and laden with
commissioned paintings, do they ever
for a moment, trip upon that old heart

so bent upon the jazz of words against words
making beauty in rhythm, sound, in twisted
clash of constructs we did not really grasp

but felt? How many poets have disappeared
into the predictability of clockwork lunches,
slick accords, persistent mortgage and spouse

and child, abandoning that clandestine affair
of teenage years? Backsliders, they abandon –
like once prodigy evangelists propped up to the pulpit

by boxes and childlike faith – the calling for
mammon. Or were they ever truly saved, born
again into the cultish itch of the poet to make

order of the disorder of our terrible existence?
Here in this tiny room of stripping plaster
the magic is relived only as an echo: the play of light on the floor.

He was remembered
his name becoming a common
noun and verb in regular parlance:

A yap

(/yap/ *n.* **yap yappist**/ya-pest/*vi*   **yap yapped** /yap-t/[Youthful innovation Jamaica College] (1974) 1: HOMOSEXUAL usually considered obscene; 2: battyman and specialist in homosexual practices; 3: the scourge of school boys; 4: their secret fear when clandestine hands cause self-inflicted sticky orgasms; 5: something no boy admits he is to other boys. (*no longer in common usage*)

A gentle boy with a sharp tongue,
he played chess quickly, aggressively
winning with a laugh – played football

in a torn yellow shirt and red shorts;
his father sold radios and calculators
in an air-conditioned appliance store

somewhere downtown and made good money.
They lured him into the piss-stink toilet
flooded with loose water and shit,

its blue walls scarred with obscenities,
secrets about teachers, yearnings,
hieroglyphics of a twisted culture.

Nunez, the short Syrian, was the bait
with his tight pants and benign smile;
securing his heterosexual credentials

despite his lisp and delicate eyes.
They lured Yap into the toilet
where he thought he'd find a friend.

They beat his head till blood
washed the soaked cement floor
and his blue shirt turned purple.

This dizzy day of crows circling
heating to a haze the old cream buildings,
and lonely on the feet-worn dust

under the tamarind tree
sat Yap, wiping the blood
from his broken teeth,

tears streaming, frantic to find words
to explain why he wanted to leave
this school and why his shirt was wet

like that. The Citroen sailed in
and stopped. The door opened, swallowed
Yap. The Citroen sailed out.

SEX SELLS ANNETTE

i

Acrobatic automatic waist control –
she could wind up a trip
in two minutes like that.

Then sipping on a cigarette
she counts her money, begging
the worn-out embarrassed man

to walk out the back way
so she could get some sleep.
Annette Sex Sells, the Deputy,

forgets what coming is like
with a man. On Monday she had
an argument with herself

because she could swear
that under the Prime Minister's
panting ministrations she felt

that old feeling of water welling;
and she started to make the right noises,
but in retrospect, after lying down

with ganja smoke and syrup
running through her head like balm,
it seemed like nothing, and she

sure she was pretending again. She couldn't ask
the Prime Minister, basking in his primal glory beside her –
you know what he would say.

have to know
to work it
like art

can't overdo it
have to work it
syrupy slow

nothing rushed
smooth out
the jerk

think round
think velvet
working it

hard like that
on nutsford
boulevard.

iii

Sex Sells
collects shells
on her dressing table

covered up in yellow
crochet with tiny bells
dangling from the edge.

It smells
of sea and dry fish
roasting in the cradle

of coals and coral.
Soldier-crab shell —
flash of blue and red

like technicolour lightning
flashing over the delicate thin membrane —
lifted to the light,

the lines move.
The soldier-crab was naked
when Annette captured his home.

She didn't kill him, just plucked him out and tossed him
brandishing his claws like a fist full of knives
in the swallowing black sand.

She backed back and watched
the seagull wail and dive.
Bye bye, soldier-crab; so life go.

iv

Spiralling home,
Sex Sells Annette still hearing
her voice in the clamour of women

screaming, 'More slackness, Shabba!'
Guinness splashing her good red blouse,
her waistline mindless of the dangerous

war it playing with physics.
And lizard-head Shabba with a voice like crocodile roar
and a tongue like a fist, dish out the slackness

like a banner of red over the trembling crowd.
And Sex Sells Annette let her eyes close
feeling the bass-line beating against her breasts.

The men stand on the edges like harbour shark – mouth watering,
teeth bright like star – urging Shabba on with the foreplay,
waiting for the moment to slide in place

behind the blind winding of some daughter
too wash down with sweat and fire
to care who she masquerading with.

Spiralling home,
the road tilting like a wall of light,
Sex Sells Annette can't tell the sweat from the blood;

the stout in her head and the ganja numbness
from the cut soaking up her two hundred dollar perm;
and her good red blouse shining in the street light.

v

They show respect 'cause
it's not what you do with them
but how you do it and whose bed

you was on when you do it.
For a joke she said hello with a shoulder caress
and a wildness giggle like a baby

to the man in his tie and bank suit
with a nice pair of shoes and a Miami
wife to boot in the Plazas, and she know

that a fight break out after she pass –
her yellow shorts and shining black boots
causing havoc in their wake.

Just flexing.
Make sure things not too rusty.
Powa!

The propellers undress the sea;
the pattern of foam like a broken zip
opening where the bow cuts the wave

and closing in its wake. The seals bark.
Gulls call and dive, then soar loaded with catch.
The smell of rotting salmon lingers over the Bay

of Fundy, like a mortuary's disinfected air;
fish farms litter the coastline;
metal islands cultivating with scientific

precision these grey-black, pink-fleshed fish.
In the old days, salmon would leap up the river to spawn,
journeying against the current. They are

travellers: When tucked too low searching for
undertows to rest upon, they often scrape
their bellies on the sharp adze and bleed.

Now watch them turn and turn
in the cages waiting for the feed of
colourised herring to spit from the silver

computer bins over the islands of sea farms,
and General, the hugest of the salmon,
has a square nose where a seal chewed

on a superfreeze winter night when
her blood panicked and almost froze.
Jean Pierre, the technician and sea-cage guard,

thinks they should roast the General in onions
and fresh sea water. It is hard to read mercy
in his stare and matter-of-factly way.

He wears layers, fisherman's uniform,
passed from generation to generation:
the plaid shirt, the stained yellow jacket,

the ripped olive-green boots, the black
slack trousers with holes, the whiskers
and eye of sparkle, as if salt-sea has crystallised

on his sharp cornea. He guides the boat in;
spills us out after our visit with a grunt and grin
willing us to wet our sneakers at the water's

edge. The sun blazes through the chill.
The motor stutters, the sea parts, and
then zips shut and still.

Stunned by their own intake of poison,
the salmon turn belly up on the surface;
then sucked up by the plastic piscalator,

they plop limp and gasping in the sunlight.
One by one the gloved technicians
press with their thumbs the underside of the fish

spilling the eggs into tiny cups
destined for the hatchery, anaesthetised eyes
glazed shock on the steel deck.

They know the males from the females:
always keep them apart, never let seed touch egg,
never let the wind carry the smell of birthing

through the June air. Unburdened now the fish
are flung back in – they twitch, then tentative
as hungover denizens of nightmares, they swim

the old Sisyphean orbit of their tiny cosmos.
The fish try to spawn at night
but only fart bubbles and herring.

On the beach the rank saltiness of murdered salmon
is thick in the air. Brown seaweed sucks up the blood.
The beach is a construction site of huge cement blocks

which moor the sea-cages when tossed eighty feet down.
They sink into the muddy floor of the bay and stick.
There is no way out of this prison for the salmon,

they spin and spin in the algae-green netting,
perpetually caught in limbo, waiting for years before
being drawn up and slaughtered, steaked and stewed.

And in the morning's silence,
the sun is turning over for a last doze,
and silver startles the placid ocean.

Against the grey-green of Deer Island
a salmon leaps in a magical arc,
slaps the metal walkway in a bounce,

and then dives, cutting the chilled water on the other side.
Swimming, swimming is General (this is my fantasy)
with the square nose and skin gone pink with seal bites,

escaping from this wall of nets and weed.
General swims up river alone,
leaping the current with her empty womb,

leaping, still instinct, still travelling
to the edge of Lake Utopia, where
after so many journeyings, after abandoning

this secure world of spawning and living
at the delicate hands of technicians,
after denying herself social security and

the predictability of a steady feeding
and the safety from predator seal and osprey;
after enacting the Sisyphean patterns of all fish,

here, in the shadow of the Connors Sardine Factory
she spawns her progeny of air and dies.

AKWABA

For Sena

i

Brown snow lines the roadways.
The still, grey city whispers

in the sunrise, inching into bloom.
I see your slick wet head

swaddled in a sheet of blood
your mother breathing into the half-light.

Sena! Wailing across my heart!

ii

Lorna stares at the television
not recording the flicker of lights

just willing love to flow slow
in warm streams of her milk

into your quick-suck mouth
locked on like a fish in passion.

iii

Picture this my heart's solace:
forever, I will watch your eyes

blaze through my dim, lensless blur.
Forever, sweet Sena,

Gift from God Almighty
Akwaba, akwaba, akwaba.

MRS. LANGSTON AND THE LIVE OAK TREE

In this sandy earth, scraggly grass and sun,
a live oak tree overhangs the baseball diamond
now unruly with neglect.

The soil is stale red like somebody's been sucking the blood
from below. The live oak's been weeping for years
at the rope scar on her lower branch like a bracelet.

Mother Langston watches the live oak till she grows eyes
and they talk, telling each other of the loves lost
and the sharp pangs of arthritis in the wrist sometimes.

'Comes with age,' she says. 'Age and sin.'
And the live oak nods and complains of the pain
that chews at her lower branch.

'They said it would grow over, heal, said I was still young then,
but on cold nights, it hurts. Then comes Hugo with his arsenal
of wind and junk slapping up on me so hard;

and all I could think was: "Praise the lord!
praise the lord! Amputate the little bugger, Hugo.
If thine eye offend thee, pluck it out!

Amputate the sucker, I don't want it no more;
this arm where the weight of a too thin
fourteen year old weighed, hanging there,

hurts like a ghost arm."'
                    'Age and sin,' Mother Langston repeats.
'Uhuh. But Hugo comes and he goes. Only toyed with me,
raised some feelings and danced away like that.'

And some nights when the moon is a fingernail,
the live oak calls to Mother Langston
to come watch the lovers wrestling there under her leaves

like a tease. And they take it in stock still
like that. After, they smell the sex in the wind.
There is blood on the discarded condom – seed abandoned –

and trails of thin brown hair lace the scarred trunk
among balls of tight black hair. The red earth sucks up the spill
and the lovers – black man and white woman – cover
      their privates.

'Where is the voice in the wind?' asks Mother Langston, thinking
      of Hugo's hot
breath on her gnarled wrist. But they think it is God calling,
and they gather their travesty and flee.

Sometimes these two hear in waves the handclaps
the tears and cheers of believers revelling in Sunday bright
Sunday: pennies dropping, pennies dropping, over the red sky,

with the choir singing like a dream, like time is not moving:
'Nobody, nobody, nobody knows, nobody knows
my trouble... The troubles I've seen follow me all my days.

Glory hallelujah!'
           And Mother Langston walks to the window
and pulls darkness in with the blinds, the voices of church
stealing away soft-soft. Then she rocks like that

touching the scar where the rope cut deep.
She talks soft to the live oak rustling now in the wind.
She keeps asking for a glass of water for the heat.

GRACE

Sabbath breaks with the swish and plop
of leaping salmon, pressing against the slush
of river bend, bloated with seed and egg.

Elated by her crazy muscle and fin
she tries to fly across the bow, but plats
on the slippery deck among the tackle, rope and rubber.

Scaled, the salmon's belly is soft,
the knife parts the blue black skin
spilling viscera – this riot of blood animated

like the bubbles of air breeding in the wake
of the cutting propellers plow through the sea.
We salt the tender flesh in the Bay

and bake her dripping lemon and honey
on an abandoned rock beach. And on this blue
ecumenical morning we break red flesh

with bread on our scaled knees, eyes glazed
with gratitude. The sun settles above
the upturned cone of pine trees; the hill

for a moment is black, and then light
washes its slopes with tender green.
For what we are about to receive . . .

Amen.

poems from

PROPHETS

PROLOGUE

To write her I construct enigma
in my leaping metaphors, for the
poem dictates its own logic and

mystery. I have an investment
in this tale – she is the prophetess
whose finger, pointed, stirred bumps

on my flesh; she is the voice that
spoke my name while I sat, eyes closed
in the congregation, secure as

victim, broke and hungry as never
before, my stomach growling;
maybe it was the cake of tears

in my eye-corner that she saw,
or the sway of my broken body
which made her prophesy my need,

but the miracle of gifts offered,
the promise of a meal and debts paid,
made doubt a sin of ingratitude.

It is this my priestess of the pure,
whose eyes I dared not look into
for fear that my constant indiscretions

would be seen and revealed,
this daughter of holiness who fell
so impossibly hard into the thighs

of unbelievers, it is she whose poem
now translates itself here. And I
confess my reluctance to let her go

as she was, blue dress and white head-tie
in the corner of the room,
with a soft voice that never

lifted beyond the drab monotone,
whose every movement was a sign.
Here, in yet another

of my squalid indiscretions,
having forgotten the overwhelming
sweetness of control over the elements,

the dialogue with the supernatural,
having forgotten the security
of sinlessness, the sure path

of daily guidance of the spirit
turning in my head – turn left
or right, go forward or back –

here, in this barren city of silence,
I reach for her tarnished flesh,
pull back, afraid to be found out,

and then dare to imagine her coupling
in the blackness of the beach,
her coming, that same mouth

saying, 'Harder, harder, harder.'
I am seeking clues, some explanation
that will reveal the sleight-of-hand

of this fundamentalist miracle,
something to make me look
better than a gullible fool.

And yet, from a ladder in the clouds,
her memory descends mysterious
and miraculous in its detail.

This poem shapes its own peculiar metaphors,
its own demanding regimen of faith,
and Clarice the prophetess glows the more.

I know now that she did have wings,
brilliant multicoloured plumes
that lifted her above the squalor and muck.

CHAPTER I

Introit

Goats chewing almond seeds
daub their sweat into the pale blue wall;
they scamper from the congregation coming

in a wave of perfumes and too much cologne,
in casual brights and patent leather,
bibles tucked like swords under their arms.

Clarice's make-up is minimal; the mascara
thin under the red eyelid. She is in
reverie. The visions are already spinning.

In her blue chiffon dress and white head-tie,
she carries her virgin body like a saint,
the prayers turning in her bright morning eyes.

It is the journey there that torments her,
through the poverty and squalor beyond the wall
separating this hibiscus-red avenue from the shack

and shingle of the spreading ghettos
where her father's dust-worn blackness fades
into the shadow and grey of the smoke yards.

Head forward, it is the reaching only that she sees.
Her mantle of importance is her light. 'Good mornings'
are guarded; the brothers keep their righteous distance.

The slick 'off-the-wharfs' car breathes in Sunday morning's
blossoming. Poinsettias bleed
on the riot of green. It is the birthing season,

and pregnant sisters pray for a Christmas baby.
The brothers who have come to pick her up
and carry her to the gathering know she will

flail them with her revelations of their straying souls,
so no foul imaginings enter their fertile minds
on the slow drive through Kingston's satellite suburbs.

Clarice stands in the spill of shade and light
of the sprawling mango trees which darken the old grey
cement, the leaning tombstone of the Castleberrys,

white landed aristocrats with their St. Andrew
lilt of an accent, who called their souls
Jamaican years before the slaves had Africa ripped

from their dreamings and heaven flights.
Sunday strolls casual as this magic of ghosts
wavering in the light dispersal of seed.

The brothers recite their verses to ward off
the lust, seeing Clarice like that, her curve of breast
and wet, dipped lips, the glow of moistness

on her ochre soft face. The rolled-down windows
temper the bite of her perfume, and the car noses
silent through the wrought gates, into the city's

Sunday dream. All in silence past the
antennae of steel and metal of the madman's
shrine on Hope Road, they eye his red daze

and say a prayer for his tormented soul. Too late
now to stop for the casting out of demons; the congregation
is waiting, and Clarice is never late.

The gravel driveway is strewn with goats'
droppings of olive green and black;
cane trash sucked dry-dry and coconut husks

litter the parking lot, spilling from the grilled
doorway of the Guild Building. In the air the stale renk
of spilt Red Stripe, curdling vomit, ganja and

sweat is thick as in the drifting carcass of an old slaver
after the liberation of the encumbered souls.
This is the hangover of Saturday night's rites of carnival

release before the righteous glare of Sunday penance:
that slow deliberate march to the chapel door
where the congregation rocks its own lamentations.

Inside, the tiles are slippery with brown glass sparkling
under the swelling sun, frothing Guinness and a yellowed
sea of spilled curried goat. Shifting mountains

of flies dance around the gnawed remains
of boiled flesh and bones, the finely grained white
rice. The goats bleat their remembrances in the yard.

Before long, the hallelujah chorus will startle
this stale cloud of carnival and the sweep of prophecies
will clear the air. With new intoxications, the congregation

will wheel and tambourine away the yawning spirits
who have overslept, hungover like this, wincing at the scream
in the electric air, the knocking of the fans

dangerously turning above the clapping and singing.
Clarice picks her way through the debris of sin
and bows in prayer while the brothers broom

the mess into mounds to be burned: pyres of sacrifice
turning in the morning air. Then, singing softly,
Clarice sirens the gathering to its worship.

CHAPTER III

Who Will Mourn for Her? (Nabum 3:7)

This Nineveh, tucked from the hurricane's blast,
riding the harmattan and lapped by the Atlantic turned foul
with the restless spirits of abandoned slaves

whose fish-gnawed bones never drifted to the broken
coastline of the rocky eastern cliffs facing Africa
all along the archipelago; this Nineveh city,

guarded by the wall of first defence and the decoy
of Cuba's agnostic bravado, is content and safe
in the warm thighs of the bearded Blue Mountains,

thumping with the wave-rock of the dip and sweet fall-back of
dancehall and gravel-voiced djs proclaiming
the new sound, the new prophecy of slackness.

The men feel for their airy crotches on the corner,
crawling from door to door discarding their progeny.
The women grind on the rain-slick street corners,

batty-riders wilding it up in the lewd light,
or lean their overflowing bosoms over the balconied
mansions of Beverly Hills, contemplating the new hunger

with its pragmatics of finding the right price every time.
Infidels skank to the visionless platform
of sweet-mouthed politricksters looking a contract

for their twilight years on the stump, rubbing 'risto shoulders
with the muck and blood of the ghetto – this
is retirement time, and every Christ is fixing

a tidy nest up in the sky for the greying times.
As the salt sea breeze catches the scent of the hull –
the rusty manacles, old red iron, the indelicate

farts of the souring bellies – head up always,
the worms crawl from their hovels at night,
watching for the quick stealth-dive of the gull.

They, insomniac in this new evolution of nature,
eyes bright infra-red darts, find the soft heads
and, quick bobbing, beak the crawlers.

ii

In this Ninevite valley, where the crossroads are sentried
with hustling preachermen among the broken
forms of slow-breathing madmen, who chuckle at the spectacle

in their all-black clothes shining to ciré in the sun,
the gospel is a three-card monte, crown and anchor board,
and the preacherman's hype is rapid fire and sweat.

Amazed and exhorted, the haremed sisters spur him on,
banging their arc of tambourines for the sinners
to come home, come home, come home.

The mawga sermonizer is black like a shak-shak pod
and dry same way, his body trembling out hope
of the precious gifts of the Almighty: the visa for a soul.

The testimonies are of those who have left;
the letters, read with ceremony and solemn ritual,
betray the lingering envy for those who have gone before –

thank God for his mercy – in the excuses, the rationalising
of the mysterious ways of the Lord. A sybil mother testifies:
'Brothers and sisters, the Lord has kept me here

like Paul, for he knows there are souls like you
to be won – for I woulda be walking the streets of Baltimore
with a green card and a Bible long time, but who

was going to sing this gospel unto yuh wutliss souls?
Is not one somebody me pray over an anoint with the oil
of joy for mourning right out there so on Oxford Street,

an is not accident mek the doberman guard
smile him bruk teet an seh, "I see the glory. Hallelujah..."
An is not one somebody me pray up dem stairs

t'rough the raw smell and stink a dem ole neaga a try
defy the way of the Lawd fe de visa – People,
when time neaga a fret is a foul smell dem give off.

Me see one entry, multiple five-year visa,
me see multiple indefinite an even a green card,
an is not no saint dem, none a dem do de preachin what

this dawta of Zion do every blessed Sunday,
but dat is de way of the Lawd, and why a woman mus
bitter? De Lawd is good and fait'ful. Is me carry dem

a airport, me pay de taxi fare, me. For me not red-eye,
for I count it all joy whatever arrows the Lord
sen my way, for him nah go give me more dan what

I can bear. Amen? Amen? Amen! Amen!'
Tongues like fire in the place, and the sister holding
back the tears fire in her eyeball, heavy in her chest,

for this chastisement is hotter than anything she has known,
working down on her: varicose veins and the gas in her stomach,
the black swelling of her knuckles and knees.

iii

The poison of heaven's sudden curse
blows from Newark's phallic white towers,
spewing their toxic sperm into the fertile sky,

seeding her perpetually. She can't get enough,
they've been saying, she just lies there and takes it all,
then she lifts her skirts and blows south for the sun

across the Bahamas sky, too high for Haiti to see,
and then over Jamaica she aborts again.
 Her rain of gaudy wetness jewels the beaches,

and the natives cough up blood and yellow phlegm,
balancing deftly the tropical rum punches on trays
through the sheets of tanning flesh on Morgan's deck.

In the shadow of an abandoned storefront
on Harbour Street, a squatting madman
shits his last meal with heartfelt reluctance

before the patient mongrel who has been
following for days for this repast.
This is the Ninevite valley

where on the hills the proffered open palms
of white satellites catch the passing rays
beaming-in a diet of soaps and family-value sitcoms.

69

Soon they are welcoming the swooping helicopters
with their marines and prospectors
with a satchel of visas, a constitution, a capitol hill.

'We will fly Dixie high if it's all we have to pay;
allegiance is a marketable commodity to us
ultimate merchants; we learnt a lot on the auction block.

Note the stump; our feet are impressed in it still.
We fit snug into the old mould, now new world order.'

Seen from the bearded Blue Mountains

the valley shimmers like a bed of gems,
and the feet of the descending prophet, dusty with travelling,
hesitate as the air changes. The mint and pine

of the upper slopes are steaming into the humidity
of the million pyres glowing in the yards.
The feet shift, then stop.

CHAPTER VI

Denial

i

Deny it as she may, as she does,
denial three times over, denied
her nose, a fist of fired black clay

on her round bones and gummy flesh,
the heavy eyelids, now wrinkling,
the peppered coil of her hair, ropes

hanging in plaits over her broad brow,
this woman is black as burnt mahogany.
Africa clogs thick in her tongue

now twisting around King James' syntax
with her own stress and relax;
but her bleeding Christ has crystal blue eyes,

(to suggest otherwise would be sacrilege)
and her water-walker is clad in whiter-than-snow
seamless expensive threads,

(don't ask her not to covet the good things
in life, or not claim her bounty
as any child of a king should).

This sybil, in her white frilled blouse
stretched taut over the coarse starch
of her boned brassiere, she denies

her lips, her rocking waistline,
the way it lifts and turns, all buttocks,
balancing her sway to the bass-line

of the huge tambourine she batters
her yellow calloused palms'
rapid rhythm, and the brilliant light

of the tiny cymbals dancing in her head,
as the congregation bursts, all reverie,
all spastic shudder to the entering spirit.

Denying still the Africa of this meeting,
exorcising the suggestion of the word,
she prays for the noble missionaries

who have left the security and nostalgia
of their snowed-in Minnesota ranch to risk
being stewed in groundnut paste.

But how can I watch my grandmother
transported like this into the congregation,
hymning her lament, and not see her ululating near the river

where the boys shed their circumcision blood;
not see her journey along the coast
caped in its red scarf of sunset bleeding

over the drag of pebble at the surf's retreat —
here in this Elmina suburb, overlooked by the castle
where the bones grope blindly for missing joints;

not see her deftly pounding the pestle,
her green and black print cloth tucked high
up her tree-trunk thighs, thumbing the sweat

into the red dirt of this Akan coastal valley;
not see her leading the grandchildren through the bush
to the plot where she hoes the earth, turning over

the blanketed cassava among the scamper of
neurotic red ants? Deny as she may,
this sybil, corseted by her circumstance of birth,

she is still St. Thomas soil, black Maroon mother
with the curse of nigger in her rolling gait.
And though the fervid sermons have scrubbed

the moss from her skin, they have found
not pink, not whiter than snow,
but flesh red and tender as a wound.

ii

I will garland you in kente and bandanna your
mystery head with the queen's cloth,
despite your protests and curses;

and in your dreams I will plant not
Toronto's blue sterility, where you will lie huddled,
old black woman coming to take another job,

and die with a visa and a social security card (for what?)
but the cool misty hills of Kilimanjaro's
piedmont greenery, where your yam will

twine about bamboo supports, and the nights
will gather in falling clouds across the
purpling skyline. In this dream, the youth

will journey the thirty miles on foot
to the kraal where you will anoint their heads
and speak your whispered conferences

with the one who comes from the lofty rock face
with a satchel of eternal truths ribboned
in cryptic proverbs and antiphonal song.

For though our heaven may be all nostalgia and created myth
it is my gift to you, sybil, while you sleep
to the symphony of gunshots in the tenement.

CHAPTER IX

Confessional

i

'My damning fantasy, what cling to my brain
like bloodstain, a follow me like a hungry mongrel,
can' shake it off, can' turn it back...'

Last Night begins, in the white kitchen.
Clarice, domestic confessor of the wayward,
cuts the heads of skellions with quick

taps of the blade on the formica counter.
'Is a bad drunken woman, one who can talk
nasty about what she want a man fe do her;

a black woman with bold bright eye
smelling a talcum and sweet perfume
with old carbolic in the mix somewhere,

Lord forgive me.' Clarice scoops the chopped
vegetables in her shining hands, green and orange
with slick wet tomatoes, and spills them

into the exploding dutch-pot oil; the onions
brown their crisp sweet smell in the room;
the radio plays Maxi Priest.

'An she can dance the bogle, with her knees
supple as guava switch, an everything so tight
that her back just a sweat an shine,

an her waist is like a pivot, an her batty bang
out like a Somali baby belly, shining crescents
under her frayed denim shorts.' Clarice's back's

to him, her sexless body in a cotton shift
motionless, her two dusty sandals shuffling.
'An she don't wait for me to say what I want,

for she tipsy and bold, an she just want an want,
she smile her red smile, dear God, an her bad eye
tumble down pon me, an take it like that.

An all de while is pure slackness from her mout
a slap me one side an the nex wid her stinking word
dem. Forgive me, saviour – ah can just smell

the sweat and wetness. Why it won' leave me, sister?
After all is not lickle pray ah pray, but she jus
a come back.' The sharp pricks in his groin

torment. He can't stop now. 'Tumble down
on me, like that. Is wine she been drinking,
an it sour in her mout, an she jus taking an

taking what she want, all she want, everything, her hip
jusa ride an a turn... God forgive me, but is the truth,
Sister Clarice... Is like a bad dream, Sister. Won'

lef me, the way she abuse me, the way she shame me,
the way she jus mash me up dereso till she get
what she want, till she bruk with a piece a shouting

like she vex wid me. Then she just lif up herself,
draw up her garments an step over me so.
Not even a tank yuh, piece a dog shit, nothing.

An me shame like a dog with me something still
a stan up same way, no release in sight. So
me abuse myself, Sister Clarice, for what a man mus do?'

Clarice turns from the saltfish fritters
and slaps him pepper and onion across the face.
Falling in shock against the fridge,

his eyes water, his teeth cut his cheek.
She marches away with dramatic hissing teeth,
the oil still popping in the dutch pot.

Yet, through the haze, to his shame, he imagines
her hips swaying with too much accent,
her tightly-girded loins trembling.

CHAPTER XV

Legion

i

A camera metaphor must be engaged
for this *mise en scene*. Pragmatic Judas
stands in the crystallised salt on the deck

there on the Galilee Sea and mutters,
'Is that not a patent waste of good
fresh pork? The Gentiles like it jerked

in pimento and ginger, soaked like that
for days with a touch of their brown
slave sugar. They pay good money for

this – and what of the poor hog farmer?
You see him leaping hallelujah on the
craggy stones, frightening the wild gulls?

I won't even mention the rights of the pigs.'
To catch this kosher miracle,
this parable in sacrificial slaughter,

close in tight on a gnarled finger, (use a red
tint to avoid conferences, subcommittees,
Trent-like councils debating His complexion)

cut to the frothing chap – filth like a second
or third skin and a distinct madness in
his eyes. This you will see from the quick

zoom-in: red eyes darting. Forget sound;
the image will blow your mind with its own
music. Then the startled scream, no mouth,

no source, just this curling surround-
sound and hear the sharp intake of breath
in the zombied theatre. Pan now, pan

so fast the olive grove is a blur, the
ochre rocks a line of reddish yellow,
like streaks of bird-shit across

a windshield with stupidly waving wipers,
and the plate sky seems still with the
sparrow dip-winged and darting with

the pan. (You may have to do
several takes to get this right.) The pigs
must look like hogs, swine even,

chomping some old carcass in the suddenly
bleak day, blood indeed, and slimy viscera
when the camera pan stops. Then, as if startled

by this glare of the camera,
(which, you well understand now, contains
the legion of stirred-up demons who

scream like kids on a roller coaster ride,
wild expletives mingled with laughter and
the subtle smell of loose shit) the swine will run! In their mud

and blooded jowls, the swine will stump and
stumble, as the camera, handheld and
unstable, follows the piggish stampede,

wild screaming stirred by a few choice
off-camera blows (the disclaimer in the credits
will silence the SPCA), and tumble, tumble,

keep that pan moving until the cliff
edge where a stampede camera
catches the flap of teats and hog balls

leaping into the churning sea. Ahhh!...
This miracle is only complete when
the cut-away returns to the man

now robed in symbolic white, his hair
a tad cleaner (they expect this – bluff it)
and Christ grinning. 'Whose blasted swine

were those? Ever thought of what
all that rotting pork and chemical run-off
could do to the fragile ecosystem?'

This is an optional voice-over
for the cynics. Otherwise wash it with the strings
you always wanted to use. This is

a demonstration of the drama's importance
in these things. The converts will come, seen
this way. It is not extraordinary.

We see it again and again. The wind picks
up on the sea and the waves lurch
steep and high. The man is taking off

His sandals. He does not mind
His feet getting wet a bit. Do not try
to add this to the film, miracles are hard to fudge.

Trick photography appears cheap and tacky
and the mystery is the thing, after all.
But a solid parting shot is everything:

Picture in medium frame, but colour sharp,
the ex-insane arguing animatedly
with the swine herdsman about the hogs;

then a long shot with the tip of the ship's bow
cutting into the chop of the sea, with Christ,
arms open against the tumbling storm,

white robes flapping in the wind,
his hair like gold ribbons in the greying sky;
then the chopper shot: the swooping eye

of the steady-cam panning the wrinkled sea surface.
Then, pulling back, see mountains and blue sea,
and the boat bobbing in miraculous light: sunset.

CHAPTER XXII

from *The Saints Return Triumphant*

i

There is rejoicing in the pews this morning,
bright arcs of tambourines. The children of perdition,
faces black with the Nile's sun, are transported

in their sudden awakening to a stretch of Gaza
in the shelter of pyramids and the sphinx,
kicking up hot sand like sojourners

after the parting of the waters, after their arrival
in this fertile land of salvation. Oh, they have seen
the work of the Lord, and there is rejoicing in the pews.

There is leaping in the hall of light this morning,
spirited dancing among the saints, for the Lord
has triumphed in his holy ways, and good tidings

make their healing path through the swaying believers.
Displayed like the spoils of war, the new believers stand
in chain-link order, freshly heaved from the black water

of St. Thomas in the East. How the mighty have fallen,
how piously reverent glow these newcomers to light,
eyes still blinking, mouths still gasping for air.

ii

Myrtle, the prostitute from Annotto Bay, grins
her puss eyes, her assets concealed beneath white robes.
What magic purrs beneath the swoop of her garments?

Watch her spin like a gig unleashed, her feet blurred.
In this frenzy, all is gloriously hot; tears mingling with sweat
as Myrtle, redeemed, torments her soul on the thrashing floor.

Sandra, the nyah queen of her mountain village,
has shorn her locks and holds the long snakes
of black and silver in outstretched arms, like an offering.

Note the twitch in her tight jaw, the glaze of her eyes,
while believers gawk at this immaculate sacrifice,
as if the snakes will suddenly uncurl and attack.

Seeing, she is drinking in, gulping, her visions unleashed;
her tight neck flexes in quick spasms, as her head,
sweat clean, but unruly like the patches of a mangy bitch,

bobs and weaves, evading the jabs of the evil one.
She is skipping to the thump and syncopation of hymnals;
tongues of fire come flaming from her opened mouth.

Broad-mouthed Merle, who sprinkled her dust at the feet
of God's messenger and gathered her invisible zombies
to hurl stones from the sky while the Holy Ghost

wrought his magical glory in the twilight of the beach's
recline; Merle, whose finger could crook a grown man
to the floor, grovelling like a croaking lizard to her beck;

Merle, the power that be, poised against the wind
with her satchel of plagues and pestilence; Merle, standing in line,
captive sister of the crusading Clarice, now caught in glory,

is giddy with this new reckoning. For power like that
which she has seen at the hands of the prophetess
is power to bring supplication. These impossible occurrences,

treasured in the hearts of the people who chuckle at cynics
and their scientific quest for evidence, have brought
the heave and chaos of thanksgiving in the pews this morning.

iii

Clarice, with face glowing, as if returned
from the encounter on Mount Sinai,
oversees the rejoicing with her quick eye.

Her spoils of spiritual warfare displayed
like undulating trophies before the congregation:
he who has eyes to see, let him see.

Last Night stares stone-faced at the improbable
lauding of his exploits in battle. The congregation
translates this as the heavenly glare. None cross him.

He remembers the sting of salt, the pull of sand,
the prick of pebble and stone on his nakedness,
the sharp cold of the new wind on his startled skin;

in his throat is the howl of the madman
dashing along the fresh beach stark as birth,
waiting for the wrath to fall.

iv

She who has ears to hear, let her hear
the hallelujah chorus; see the dancing brothers,
sweat pouring, clothes sticking to their torsos,

as they leap naked in the eyes of the maidens of God:
David before Michal and her nun's pout and frown,
each leap a contest to touch Jehovah's

83

proffered hands. The congregation trembles
in relayed plosives, the babble of unknown tongues
washing the witnesses with impossible love.

v

Returned from the dense mist of St. Thomas in the East,
returned intact from the stronghold of Satan
and his minions of falling lights, returned unbroken,

returned triumphant, let the church say amen.
Returned with song: Can I get a witness!
Returned with feet still skipping: Glory!

Returned with captivity captive: Yes!
With the chains of degradation broken asunder: Uhuh!
With the faith intact despite the perilous way!

Returned with a song of triumph on the lips!
Returned with a song of victory on the lips!
Returned, returned, returned!

A flurry of clapping shatters the stoic resolve
of Last Night who, leaping like one unburdened,
hurls his body into the waves of fire.

Clarice, at the pulpit, collapses in her stomach
for her lover has found his feet again.
Her tears soften her path like scattered roses

at the feet of one who comes with blessings and with joy;
she gathers his broken self to her bosom
and rocks him whimpering there in the whirl of tongues.

from CHAPTER XXIII

Thalbot and the Vine

i

At the cliffs, the wind
carves its caves of eyes and gaping mouths,
the echo of last night's storm still

lingering like after-death. Thalbot hears the Lord,
'Go! Go!' He speaks in the waves and the wind,
for this is the chronicled manner of his presence.

'Go to the city where the wickedness of Sodom
is a tattered coat on their backs; you will know
them by their decadence. Tell them you have seen

the arc of my holy sceptre falling. Avoid proper
names, stick to pronouns breathed with reverence –
such aspirants from your lungs will carry fire –

this I promise. I thrive on enigma, names spoil the effect,
use symbols and pronouns. I'll do the rest.
Tell them that the light of the sky will pour

a hail of fire into their broken upturned cups.
Speak this compelling prophecy like a naked mad man
in the streets and, if you must, eat grass, chew

laboriously, regurgitate, relish the green juice.
They will understand; it has been done before.
Tell them of the brilliant impossible you have witnessed

in the churchyard these last few nights, tell them
of the prospect of these truths unfolding
like a yellow banner across the dark.

I only ask that you carry my salvation
into the heart of the City.' This is how the Lord
comes to Thalbot's trembling brain.

But how can he go like this, faithless
and blinded? How, after witnessing the preacherman
and the prophetess coupling like dogs on the beach?

How, after his own vicarious coming, voyeur
without the strength to look away? What is
left but this heaviness, this pull to the edge,

to the bosom of the sea where the gravel sand
and picking fish would cleanse all mortality
from his fallen flesh, where death at sea by drowning

would be cool and silent among the shell and coral?
This dying would salvage the possibility
of hope. But the voice of God is in the wind,

and visions spread across the lapping ocean in
coloured cinematic panorama. There lies the sore
of the Caribbean as midnight acolytes of worms

snake through the narrow avenues to the sound
system's call, arms tossed high in spastic animation,
the wind whipping the stench of their carelessly

dropped defecation into the air. This is the vision
spread over the ocean, and the voice of God in the wind
shouts, 'Go! Go! How can you not go?'

ii

Thalbot's reluctance is understandable.
Remember, this is his city and home,
and Belleview, dusty and hot by the sea,

is his former residence, rising
above Seaview's gangrened streets,
their potholes seeping brown and caking at the edge,

Belleview, where the doctors perform casual experiments,
opening the gates of the patients' brains
while the fans turn the sweat and farts,

circulating nothing new, just the same smells.
How to speak of salvation to the stone-throwers,
the laughing women, the teenage girls with

their startled curiosity devouring his blatant shame?
How to preach into the broken vessel where gunmen
practice marksmanship on the dizzy madmen,

and the whores urinate and spit, taking out their
resentments on the madmen's drooping heads, as the
volvos, all rolled-up and chilling, cruise by?

Oh let the stones fall off the mountains
on this city of lapsed nyabinghi and renta-dreads.
Let old Zion fire cut through the brittle

wharfs and flame its way up the hills,
gutting the mansions and the jewelled slopes
flowering their satellites like rusting white

chrysanthemums, that catch the seed
from the Beast jerking its self-assured self
off over the Basin. This fire will leave the earth

black with nutrients and chemicals where fresh
living soil can birth new truths, new mercies.
This is Thalbot's hope, the rationale for his

flight in the other direction. For what right has a city
to live again when the prophet himself is blind,
when he has seen and cannot remove the vision

of the preacherman and the prophetess howling
in their coming? And she with her proffered bottom,
what miracle is left in the seduction of her slow

casual walk back to the chapel doors, while the
preacher tries to swallow the black ocean into his
fevered soul, sobbing like that? Fall is all. Silence

the only answer. The wind grows still, having spoken,
and Thalbot hurls the words over the sea
but they do not splash as they fall, they float.

iii

He lifts his soul and leaps over the rocks,
over the cactus and tangle of sea-grape trees
into the somnolent mainstreet, down

to the junction where a small party of travellers,
three tourists, two dreads,
and four top-flight Annotto Bay whores,

have gathered around a mini-van to journey
to Montego Bay to see Shabba and the Cat.
There is the sweet aroma of cherished colly in the air

and the van is rocking to rapid-fire synthetic
bass-lines. Negotiating his escape calmly,
Thalbot offers a red hundred dollar and climbs

into the depth of the van. One of the women
presses her softness into his side, and laughs
lightly, drawing him into the herb on her breath.

He laughs, falling into the sway of the rocking
van, the reggae trembling the loose windows.
He knows he is being watched like the sparrow.

He closes his eyes trying to forget the prophecy,
trying to quiet his bleating soul, and the van
prods its way along the coast towards Montego Bay.

iv

At Joppa the tyre explodes on a curve that
overlooks the gullied cottage of a gentle country
woman. The ferns on the hill face

drip dew; a river flowing from the rock
gurgles beneath the asphalt bridge
and spills into the lazy sea.

Disgorged in giggles and gentle expletives,
the people squat in the moonlight, eyes
glazed with the back twist of the herb,

while the driver sweats on a new wheel,
cursing at the vindictiveness of it all.
Thalbot lingers in the shadows beneath

the leaning trees, watching for careering
vehicles, or bolts of unsuspected lightning
from above. But the task is completed

without event; God stays silent. Yet, after half
a mile, the exhaust falls and clanks, the chassis
breaks, the radio falls dead, the engine sputters,

the van comes to a bawling halt, and someone
mentions a curse. As if on cue, the others
find religion and search their past for a reason.

One girl announces that she has been cursed
by her obeah grandmother, who thinks it is
church she going to now. But Thalbot knows,

hearing the spirit at his back, and sees the logic
of his truth, still too far from Tarshish.
He draws the driver aside and whispers.

He offers to walk and free them of the curse,
but the driver fears to abandon a bonafide prophet
on the road, rudderless, with no hope of salvation.

The gathering grows impatient so Thalbot
walks away. The driver shifts gear and pulls
out, the red tail-light bouncing into the blackness.

Thalbot plants his left foot and uproots the right:
the walking is tedious. He still points to Montego Bay,
leaving behind the spastic madness of Nineveh.

v

Coming with the thunder of storms,
the hiss of a whale's breathing,
this cylinder of grimy seats and caution

airbrakes, riding, caressing the sudden
curves of the wavy coastline,
the driver sweating out his quart of whites,

the blue and gold forty-seater, with
a cage of soldered iron for a crown,
sways empty in the rural night.

The broken hydraulics of the side door
flap their rhythmic metallic claps
like an alarm before the cough and rattle

of the engine. The plastic glass
of the windows rattles like shak-shaks
in the leap and lurch of this dance

threading around the potholes
of the coastline. The gear brake-down
for the turn into the hills

startles Thalbot, who is waiting at the
junction for another vessel to bear him
west before the sun breaks the horizon.

Caught in the stark light and the
slow drag of the uncertain wheels,
Thalbot stands to leap but instead

is caught in a motion as helpless as the
blind stare of a jacked deer. The air
hisses, the wheels squeal as the hiccuping

bus stops. It shudders,
nose pointed to the hills and their
enclosing trees, beyond which the roads

twist and meander, beyond which spreads
the land of Nineveh, the lamentable city,
all primed for the rain of damnation from heaven.

'You will dead out hereso, boss. Man
will cut you t'roat and drink you blood.
Come aboard. The door is open. Town!'

Looking for a light, for a village with the security
of a roadside chapel, Thalbot boards
the panting bus and looks to the

silhouette of the driver, a back,
a way of leaning against the wheel,
a texture of laughter, an omen, a prophecy.

The bus lurches and swings, the lights blink,
the shadows play games on the green
hard plastic seats; there is the smell of green bananas'

sticky blood, old thick market-sweet thyme,
the sweat of the clustered souls travelling.
Throughout those lurching hours Thalbot groans on the slopes

of twisted Mount Diablo. On the striped
and blackened steel deck lie scattered,
crushed callaloo leaves and a spill

of pepper seeds. The hills come quickly
to meet the broad windshield; the
bus sits on the road and rides it out.

Thalbot watches the comfort of country
chapels hurtle by in streaks of light,
the congregations swaying in pink hues,

the Bible-bearing infants, the truth
in the steeple and bells of the facades,
but the driver, shifting gear, leaps forward.

At the top of the mountain, the glow
of Nineveh suggests itself in the sky.
Thalbot shouts to the sweating back

of the driver, but the shifting gears continue,
the blast of the horn on a chain.
The sermon in his belly sours.

The journey down into the vegetation
of the foothills is smooth, but the way
home has become uncertain.

Thalbot falls to his knees and scratches
his overheated flesh. The earth is growing
brighter in the coming dawn.

vi

'When trouble catch me, undress me,
leave me bleeding by the roadside; when
the blindness of seeing the unholy nastiness

on the beach darken me day; when the
curse of the Lord follow me from Annotto
Bay's slick street and clapping

congregation marching to the altar
and falling falling so; when the dead
arising and the cripple gyrating, and

the twist-up guava bush rejoicing;
when the prophetess riding
a new prophecy on the naked beach,

milking him, milking him;
(when last you said your prayers, woman,
when last you count your beads? Morning

coming and the thin membrane of your drying
sex will catch the sun. See the soldier crab
picking away at the charred edges) it is

the cause, it is the cause!
This my Joppa so far from Tarshish, and a
thatch and mud bed for my head,

when this duppy transport, blasting exhaust
in the air, and its coolie driver, floating on weed
an sharp whites, beckon me like a siren

and swallow me into the ribbed belly
of this steaming metal tomb, this
grave where trouble follow me. When I cry

unto the Lord t'rough what I see mek me a
soul of unclean lips and cankered eye,
who hear me cryin? Who hear me?

For when you toss me into the current,
the warm wave dem lapping lapping,
and when dead take my han, (and me,

I was not fighting,) an draw me down deep,
deep into the womb of this moist fern gully,
then drag me over the twisting road, like the coral,

black but still aglow with retained light;
when I cry out, "Is dead a dead now!"
like a prophecy, and my eye dem see

the howling preacherman, his sex
jumping in the moonlight, his soul burning,
rolling like a madman in the water,

is dead a dead now. For what must follow
the absence of faith? What but this
seaweed like a rope round me neck,

and Albert Pierrepoint and his father and
father before him holding the lever,
ready to drop me, for the judgment of heaven

done sound on the blast of this bus.
Down, down ah falling like a bungy gone crazy,
not finding the jolt, just air; down,

down Mount Diablo, to Flat Bridge, to
Maroon jungle-green, the Rio Cobre,
slipping its hiss, quiet as water, me

waiting for the whiplash, the wail,
the crack, the coolie man swaying now,
spliff after spliff giving him

a heavenly cloud. When falling like this,
who it was that bear me up,
bring me forward still breathing?

This journey stop before the Baptists Cathedral
front a Parade lignum vitae shade.
Who but the Lord coulda plan the path

to this holy temple, the wind beating through
my open mouth? Yes, Father, see me here,
flat, eating the shit and dirt, eating grass.

Free me up, Giver, and Thalbot will find
music, abandon the flesh, the madness,
drop me foot and preach. You see my card now.

Though it sound like rejoicing for miracle
what done realise, this is a transaction. You see
my collateral; take it or hang me, Giver. Amen!'

vii

And the Lord commanded the bus
and it vomited Thalbot onto dry land;
and the city grunted, then turned over.

The bus rattled around the Parade Square
saluting Marcus and the fat queen,
then vanished like magic into its own tail-smoke.

CHAPTER XXIV

Speaking for the First Time

'To speak my words would be to fracture
the wings of a myth and send it careering
to the sun-baked earth.' So said the prophetess.

'To speak this now would be to shatter
the brittle wing-bones of a myth. To speak this
now after the long silence, after the vow to keep

the tongue arrested, cleaving to the palate;
to speak this now, having been
written into a fist of power, a magical

construct with the punch of a saint;
to speak now after the holy elders have
gathered at my feet as to a goddess and presented

their offerings, their exposed hearts and secret sins,
the crumpled hundred dollar bills, the funky
handkerchief of some clandestine affair,

the poured olive oil, the fragrance and herbs,
the delicate minds teetering at the abyss,
the hunger, the dread of the creditor's knock;

to speak this now after the whore's hymen
has been so carefully sealed, after the stone has
been removed and the three day dead has stumbled forth,

after the impossibility of miracles has been chronicled,
after I have been written into myth, into character
and role model, now player, now closed icon;

to speak this now, to empty my heart to the wind,
my mind that I have forgotten, lobotomized, without
motive, without fear or frailty, without sex;

to speak this now, talking woman, gossiping
herstory, to burst the straining dam, to rebel
against the white robe of righteousness and the tightly

girded loins; to speak thus, in a voice that deconstructs
the metalanguage of God's clever narratives, would be
to fracture the vulnerable wings of a myth.

But the air is too thin here at the gate of Heaven,
and I am tired of waiting in line despite the order
of my papers, when below me the clouds beckon.

How I have longed to fall through and feel the amassed
cool of dew drops, first rain on my living skin;
to let my hair snarl its unruly self in the fingers

of the wind; to let fall, my skirt billowing,
revealing the muscle and flesh of my thighs,
the embroidery of white nylon twined in the silver

of my pubis. I am discarding the visa to Heaven,
unlocking the tongue of my imprisonment,
despite Peter's frown and the stares of the pilgrims.

But they always knew of my secret fantasies
in the pink and powder of my jewelled cage;
they all saw the red bubble of my indiscretions,

the grunt and sigh on the black beach in Annotto Bay.
The visa was a simple act of payola from the gracious
brothers whose secrets I carry in my fevered head.

So now, I fall, giving myself up for dead
and not giving a damn who goes down with me.
Now broken, my wings limping, I gladly fall,

for my mouth explodes at the rush of sound,
words tumbling forth in the thick smell of earthly
truths, tongue running wildly, shaping words,

flowering in the new sun. Falling thus, the lewd sibilants,
the orgasmic gutturals, the round voluptuous vowels:
myth falling, myth falling. It is exhilarating!'

CHAPTER XXVII

The Last Poem

... For us, all there is is trying. The rest is not our business...
(Paraphrasing Eliot)

This I heard, perhaps in a dream,
but I hoped it was the voice of God
easing up some on my burdened soul.

But it came not like the wind off the hills,
nor did the sky flame with the bloody cypher
of his finger. This was no nick-of-time bleat

of a sent ram in the thicket. Alas
these were the words of a dead poet,
with no evidence of salvation, no backative,

no promise of returns and blessings for obedience,
just the poet's flirtations with the cadence
of a god. So I sat among the roses

and chewed at the bitter leaves. The weight
of the Lord's commanding drooped my
broken head, and the leaves of the slim

volume of verse, this quartet, this clandestine fantasy, this hope
for the power of earth-makers, stone-breakers,
rustled insignificantly and impotently like a poem.

CHAPTER XXVIII

Flight

i

And when I die, I will fly. What promises you have for me?
Call it a bargain basement faith, but I have to find
something what can fit my broad hip and match my

complexion. What you have for me? When I die
my pains will be no more; I will touch clouds
damp with next week's storms, over

the cedars and pines, above the smooth green
thighs of the Blue Mountains and, when I dip like a bucket,
the water from the rocks will be cool blue.

My watertight goatskin satchel will carry
smooth stones, cooling pebbles for under my tongue
when the harmattan dries the Atlantic

air waves. I will fly over Cuba
and say a prayer for Fidel (stroking my chin), for
despite the bad press, defecting daughters, etcetera, I dig

the man for his cynic's wit and mannish ways. Look the
boat-load of criminals he liberate on Miami's
red, white and oil-blue shore, and see how blood flow –

sangre de dios – in the palmetto beachhead when each defectee
prance the golden roads with scar-face badness,
dusting the green with coke like wedding rice.

Though hesitant, I will pit-stop over Babylon,
in some third world barrio like South Carolina's low country
or them turtle-green islands where they preserve

the tongue of Africa, lodged in seed and stomach,
static magic swirling on Sycorax's fantastic Bermudes,
where black man Caliban still howls his panting heart.

Then it's east, for the cold bite hugging too tight
the Atlantic rocks. East it is, for this soulful flight,
looking, looking for soil to plant in – looking, sniffing.

East along the channels of air, warm Gabon air,
smelling the *akra*'s mellow smoothness, the sweet
kelewele, calling, calling, drawing me along the warm

currents. I'm flying east for the fleshpots
of Cairo, the sphinx, the pyramids – not home,
just legacies of gifts we have left, simple skeletons.

There on Cairo's streets, panoramas of faces
whip by like old statues of ancient times,
while the Black American intellectuals sip sweet coffee

in the cafes, retrieving their lost heritage in the colonizer's
tongue. Ah, the relics of our lost histories, the things
we have lost – seeking out a Black Atlantis so far, so far

from the conclave of huts and the circle of the griot's music
in the south, where green explodes in mountains
rising out of the brittle grit and dust of the Sahara.

Whitewashed memories are shored up in colourful texts
and clichés of a glorious race. Divided is Africa;
the Egyptians wince at the kente and dashiki.

Fly, I must, from this museum of broken dreams;
fly, I must, south to the antiphonal howls of the
Mahotella Queens, the magic of the Mokola daughters,

the flaring nostrils of the township shabeens,
speaking easy their histories in the firelight;
their eyes staring far like the Masai's gaze.

This is my dignity, this my familiar earth, this my arrival,
still damp with the dew of tomorrow's rain.
I alight without fanfare from the blue; the earth

reaches up its red fingers and sucks me, legs first,
deep into the blooming bottom-land. This yank
tautens my neck like a kite rope, my head a dignity flag.

This is my dignity, constructed by so many journeys.
Why must I stay satisfied with rumours
of old women's proverbs and the *brujo*'s sharp

recognition of healing in each weed, bush and turning
leaf? Return I must to that old shrine, now broken,
for those left behind forgot to feed the soil.

Shrine of my deepest fears, whose fingers reach
across the centuries and touch my eyes, my offspring
wrestling with the Holy Ghost found in the mountain chapel;

shrine of my deepest fears, split in my devotion
from the earth that beckons me with her smell of seed
to the new libation of blood shed for remission of sin;

shrine of my deepest fears, have you not heard that I wept
and felt the fingers on my cheek wiping, wiping;
that I have dreamed of another land, comely, home?

shrine of my deepest fears, path to my distant time,
not that path which would find me back in Jericho,
or as nigger Simon on Golgotha staring at the black sky;

shrine of my deepest fears, what wind is blowing now
to meet my uneasy mind? I feel the travail in my bones.
What do you have to offer, dare I fall open before you?

Then, land I have heard about,
will you rise before my face from the spread
of desert and thick bush, Kilimanjaro

probing the cloud cover? Is this my
Eden, my heaven? Have you something better?
Have you a truth to plant me like a tree?

ii

Culture is flux. Flux is culture. Absolute spirit.
Is spirit absolutely true? Heart is not history. Heart of stone.
Heart is the fire caught-up within my bones.

Heart is prophecy frothing to the stomp and rattle
of the gospeller's Sunday. Heart is the word spoken
so deep in the stomach, so jealously protective of my soul.

Heart is my eye peering into our collective pasts
and, finding that ancient shrine in some broken hut,
drawing me. I arrive a stranger. I arrive dead. Sleep

never comes easy, for the trees of the mountain sanctuary
rustle their hymns, calling me back, calling me back.
Flux is culture. Culture is flux. We are changing inside.

iii

The dashiki I wear is a flag.
Calls me dignified. The kente, a gift
from the Ghanaian attaché, my banner.

The sandals and the dust, my contact
with the earth. There is no burden of guilt
in my history; I will not share the blame for the callous

whip; the gospel of enslavement,
justified sardining of humanity
in our own juices, value packaged

and shipped with the blessing and guiding eye
of the all-seeing papal man; nor for the stolen gold;
the satchel of smallpox and rude disease;

the blood spilt; the betrayal and slaughter of Toussaint;
Sam Sharpe bleeding in the cane fields;
the dangling of Bogle; the black and white churches;

the rejected cornerstones falling, falling in the
black water of your hell; the silencing of my songs.
I will not be no beast of burden for you no more.

I reject twilight schizophrenia; illusions
of white Jesus with his red heart
enshrined in thorns, and his hippie

hair smoothly permed as he stands propped by
his Anglo disciples with thin, stiff upper lips;
I reject, too, the Academy of Regret;

your constant belief in the beauty and joy
of Colon's accidental landing; the perpetual admonition
to avoid the backward glance for your sake;

as if it were I facing the judgement
of salt and fire, as if I had left nothing
of beauty in the old village by the sea.

No, I will not deny the prophet with
wicked locks and a Trench Town bob
in his rhygin walk who says look back,

for that yoke is easy and the burden light,
and our legacy is more than the homelessness
of the sea – I have planted seed and it has sprouted

in this new soil, I have wailed to the hills
and my voice has returned dew soft
with clear melody and the harmony

of new trees, new brooks, new light;
the antiphonal prayers of old bones
calling me to take shelter in the green.

So there's nothing strange here;
nothing odd in my ancient garb,
and the path of my metaphors.

You have, I know, heard it all before,
and more sweetly spoken, I am sure;
but I repeat the litany to clear the table

so we may start afresh. Now, clean as I am,
plealess; now that we know the lay of the land,
offer me what you have for me – go on. I am listening.

You see, I've always known this stuff –
this stuffing of history – to be
the baggage of your sterile sermons;

secretly concealed behind those curtains
while you down the best part of the wine
after we've just dipped and sipped small;

behind your Oxford tongue, acrobatic
around that clean sermon of bloodless salvation;
locked up in some closet, all this stuff

is sitting there, and if it wasn't for that smell,
that thick muggy smell seeping through,
I would never know you had all this stuff.

iv

I have come like this to see you point me
out in my cloth from Togoland and my
raggamuffin gait. Finger me now, I don't

give a damn who sees. I won't cause no
trouble. Tell the ushers to stay cool. I will smile
'cause I come to find a path – and this won't be

a path you make, it will be a path you may offer,
then I will decide and either walk the asphalt
or ride the cobalt sky on that chartered journey back.

See me sometime as your old black ancestor
before Peter at the door, proffering her
letter of recommendation to be relayed up

the ladder to God's desk or to his well-paid
letter writers: the risen popes, paul, newton, augustine
of the burning groin. Like her, I come

like a comma to replace the closure
of your periods, screwing up the text
until the end is somewhere in the middle.

Now, tell me, what you have for me,
for this Sowetan gum-boot dancer,
this Akan mother transported like a scroll,

discovered here where the bush still parts
for her footfall, slowly marching
from the sea inland to the sound of the drum?

What you have to offer me to break this miasma
of uncertain homes? What promises can speak above
the smell clamouring behind the curtains?

You see, the path you raise your left finger to
is a false path, o false prophet. This I have
seen. My morning songs lift me beyond

the chaos of your many and twisted roads.
Flying comes so natural to me these days
as I ride this sun-full, misty morning to Heartease.

v

I am reluctant to leave it like this;
the tricks, the sin, the betrayals, as if this was all.
My journey has drawn me astray and, remiss,

I am turning to the old songs. Marley's call
from the darkness is pure light and hope
despite the countless dead by unbelief.

This song has wallowed in its grief
as if there was no music in the bright aftermornings,
no prayer caught in the mist's delicate sieve.

Now, rising up like a fisherman's weighted seine
to God, the tambourines celebrate the joy of faith rewarded,
the sickly child awakening after prayer,

sight returned to a warped cornea,
hope in a miracle of a child born intact.
How green is the island when it rains!

This song has lamented like a spoilt child,
yet how can I turn from these miracles
without tears of thanksgiving in my eye?

I write these poems with trepidation,
as if this tantrum might bring down the wrath
of the Almighty. But the prophets no longer groan

through the stinking city. Their feet skip on the mountains.
The cleansed are dancing on the hill's broken path.
Now, there is laughter and belief in mornings.

poems from

JACKO JACOBUS

A WAY OF SEEING

It all comes from this dark dirt,
memory as casual as a labourer.

Remembrances of ancestors
kept in trinkets, tiny remains

that would madden anthropologists
with their namelessness.

No records, just smells of stories
passing through most tenuous links,

trusting in the birthing of seed from seed;
this calabash bowl of great grand

Martha, born a slave's child;
this bundle of socks, unused

thick woollen things for the snow —
he died, Uncle Felix, before the ship

pushed off the Kingston wharf,
nosing for winter, for London.

He never used the socks, just
had them buried with him.

So, sometimes forgetting the panorama
these poems focus like a tunnel,

To a way of seeing time past,
a way of seeing the dead.

SEED

i

Before these poems, there was not much,
just scraps of thought and deep envy

of the giants of colonial verse
forming their twilight words so sweetly.

But the occasion asks for a celebration song,
while the curry and rice still flows,

and soberness hangs by a thread,
as the bass pumps out in the dancehall.

ii

Your glory is in what you have not done;
in what you have sometimes treated

as disposable, a mere by-product
of fleeting orgasms, to be washed away,

wiped from fingers and night sheets,
left to dry, or seep into thoughtless soil.

Your glory is in a miracle you may never
comprehend – though bravado is possible,

and metaphors of swords sheathed and
unsheathed, naked for battle, are good

for morale and for action, but this
is all false glory. Instead I can speak

of the ivory temples of your descendants,
the arrows of poison that will pierce

such lofty enemies as would not even
today hire you to clean their shit;

or speak of the tough women who will
stand like sentinels over your promise,

and guard tomorrow with antiphonal song.
Then will they speak of you as if this hovel,

smelling of stale rat refuse and rotting meat,
were some glorious temple of memory.

You, though, when you enter her conch-pink door
tonight, will not know what history

you are making, but that is not your affair.
Yours is to be the stud you are,

grind your seed deep, howl, howl, for all you
are worth, then sleep and perhaps dream of glory.

TWINS

I have never been an expert
at naming artists or identifying slides,

but this image, I am sure, I have seen in peeling
paint, of shapely, carefully voluptuous

bodies, exaggerated muscles, glistening blue
eyes – two brothers, almost in flight,

cloaks of blue and red billowing like the Renaissance,
revealing the curve of thighs and calves,

one straining to clasp the heel of the other.
This birth, with perfect light and cherubims

looking on, is bloodless, wombless. Just this
commingling of myths: the heel, the twins

attached by will, the promise of betrayals to come,
the mess of lost birthrights and the cheating of fathers,

of genocide, the blasting of human guilt, the cross
on the hill amongst the waiting crows – all contained

in this moment, a prophecy of the passion
to come. But, as I said, I can't recall the name –

Botticelli, Gregorio, Raphael, Michelangelo – I sift the art
history books for clues; an unused sketch, a detail perhaps,

but find nothing of this picture's startling verisimilitude,
the way the angels' wings grow with animal conviction

from their backs, nothing dreamed, nothing misty.
So I have constructed this for you to understand

the mortal flesh I saw, this sticky clay
taking me back to a memory of being a brother,

kicking, kicking away, trying so hard
to breathe, and fly with my ankles free.

SPIDERMAN

i

Accomplice, the mother
  skins the goat herself,

stews the domesticated meat
  and pushes him to feed

his slack-jawed father,
  eyes sheathed with age.

From the washing she retrieves
  a sweat-stained shirt

rough with twigs and weeds,
  smelling of the broken soil.

Then a raw lie,
  a big unflinching lie he speaks

till blessing comes,
  like a poem, a song.

  – Are you my son, the hunter?
  – I am your son, the hunter.

ii

He, meantime, journeying across
  the parched land, fingers still stained

with blood, dreams of thick warm broth
  made from the dripping carcass on his back.

He drinks and washes at the well
and butchers the fresh-caught meat

smelling the sweet warmth of stewed game in lentils,
so thick, so lumpy with comfort and calm to come.

Inside the shack they trade gifts,
he gives away his birthright for a ready bowl of stew,

because, standing in the open fields where he is most alive,
his only birthright is the trees, the long grass, the stars,

and who can take these from him?
He sucks the broth and laughs with nonchalance.

Spiderman gathers the words of the deed
and pockets them near his heart,

for he sees a divinity in the anointing of seed,
in the way a word takes root in season.

iii

A stair leads up to light,
angels sliding up and down the banister.

There are flat stones in the stream
trickling like silver in the moonlight.

Sweating in this light,
a wingless angel wrestles the man.

A lattice pattern of light and dark
speckles these two sweating in the dirt.

Before first light, Jacko Jacobus,
  brain ticking like a con-man, spins his web again,

catching the angel by the hip
  while the others are hauling up the stairs

before the crimson of the east
  turns to dazzling day of forgotten mysteries:

Bless me now, or I will not let go
  of your naked hip. Bless me now!

And in this way he gathers
  more words, pocketing them.

BECKY

These were her words
at the jamb of the door,

her words spurring on
the treachery of their plan

while the old man snored,
waiting to bestow his love —

the angel chewing an hibiscus twig,
waiting for the right time

to gather him up, light like spirit
and take him to his destiny.

Jacko listened with trembling heart
the taste of glory in his mouth, souring:

When I saw your father,
there at the edge of town,

looking like a king in his
fancy suit, smiling like puss,

I saw love. The man had a way
to whistle mento tunes

would make any girlchild
weep with longing. The man

draw me, Jacko, that old broken man
you see in there, with no knowing

of who is coming or who is going,
with his mouth hanging open

and only sometimes a prayer coming out
from that tired, tired soul.

That man was my champion, Jacko,
and I woulda follow him anywheres.

But time pass, bone get old,
eye get dark and mind turn sof';

and this man forget what prophecy
done come to him so much years ago,

forget that is a generation of king
and priest him seed must give forth;

forget that, and instead him look to
the flesh, the strong arm, the strong back

instead of the soul, the spirit.
When a man is dead to his memory,

then someone must guide his path.
Go inside there and take what is yours,

Jacko Jacobus, father of nations,
go inside there and take what is yours.

EMIGRANT

With nothing but a bag
pack with yam and bread,

a few coins in his pocket
to multiply into food,

Jacko board the ship for Charleston,
with not even a map to tell him where

this black liner heading,
just watching the way it leave a trail,

long and white in the soft waters,
and the way the mountains start to fade,

till nothing else was left but sea.
Jacko and the day grow dark.

Leaving behind love, leaving behind mother,
leaving behind a naked brother, red with anger,

leaving behind a father to bury himself,
a father weeping psalms of regret to God.

Find yuh Uncle Al, my brother,
and marry one of him pretty daughter dem,

den multiply yuhself, son,
till you is nothing but blood and water,

multiply yuhself, son,
so yuh inheritance might breed life.

Jacko meet a young hustler
with glitter in his eyes

talking 'bout how money easy
in the peach fields of North Carolina

and work easy for hardworking man,
and that was his only plan.

Now darting like a kite abandoned
to the wind, trying to forget that him have

a history, trying to forget there is
a place called yard, called house, called home,

when the dark embrace the ship
way out on the Caribbean Sea,

cut-off, cut-off so far from shore
Jacko toss the Bible overboard,

him hear it touch the water sof'.
The boat trundle on.

OBEDIENCE TO THE WORD

Jacko Jacobus journeys across the desert
of his shame and hurt, to find at a well

the daughter of his Uncle Al. There,
love ordained of God would sprout and flourish

among the green and white dogwood light,
in the squalor of the South Side where Al is king.

And what a wondrous welcome it is:
slaughtered pigs and barbecued flesh,

malt liquor like a river to drown all tears,
and the juke joint hopping, while Jacko droops

like a lamb to the slaughter, his seed proffered, his body
to be bound to years of hard labour for his board

and wife; issuing rocks of miracle crack
and crushed leaves of purest lambs' breath.

Leah and Rachel, the daughters, watch from the edges,
both lusting for the promise of his progeny.

PUSHER

Angelus of mercy,
Al was the Pope

walking through the squalor
of an unfeeling world.

Yes, sometimes, numbed by his stuff,
he floated among the giddy children,

bestowing vials of mercy for the pain.
At first it was not the money,

just the urge to stir the darkness
of these defeated descendants of slaves

to something more volatile,
something like the bebop madness

of Miles, Coltrane, or the crazy
dreamings of Monk the magician,

something that would make
the bossman sleep uneasy at night,

with gun loaded beneath his pillow,
his daughters strapped to their beds

for fear they might catch wind
of this jazz in the air

and go low riding
near the barracks.

It was this at first,
this way to liven the drabness

of nothing lives,
this merciful act

that got him in the business.
But missionary work don't pay the bills,

and what with babies coming from his balls,
and the pittance from the bossman

not making ends meet; and the thugs
in New York looking for expansion

into the slumbering South,
Al, the pope of Hog Town,

opened his missal and bestowed
his indulgences for a price,

while the jazz grew slow and mute
and the brothers floated through their dreams,

not touching earth, not touching nothing
on their path through the trees.

And Al prospered
before the Lord.

RACHEL

There is mothering in her eyes,
in the shape of her unseeded stomach,

in the sturdy flesh of her hips,
in the way her body smells of comfort,

in the manner of a fertile ewe
with which she moves about the house,

chewing with the patience of a mother
the food she magics into being.

She was named by a keeper of livestock:
in those days, Al saw domesticated patterns

in all human flesh – cattle, goats, sheep.
He has trained her well to grow

into her name. Jacko wants to shepherd
her into his pasture, black ram tupping Al's ewe.

LEAH

You could tell by the tegareg of her walk,
a kind of slack, bone-loose sashay,

and the unruly gallop of her uncaged
breasts, that she is staring hard,

a cow with a bull's disposition,
waiting to bolt madly into the open field.

Leah saturates the lining of her dreams
with Al's magic dust – she never slumbers

to dreaminess when she is taken
by the chemistry in her blood.

She leaps and cavorts for days
till the red has left her eyes.

The house is cleaned spotlessly,
the labours of the yard are always done,

and she bounds with a strange gaze
from task to task, her skin dry as dirt.

Jacko can see Al's anxiety at the wild
teated creature; he can tell there is fear.

Jacko searches for her missing self,
but he cannot find her softer parts.

Still, he can tell by the way she stares
that she has the capacity to devour him.

AL'S DREAMYARD

Stumbling over soft bodies and loose cloth
in Al's dream yard — Ah, Christmas wind blows!

Nothing moves, just white light and then dim
and the hiss of frying crack — Ah, Christmas wind!

Headlights spot the black beyond in quick darts
as midnight sojourners climb the bridge of the I–95.

Stoned to a dumb horny uselessness, they sit
talking trash until the shit is ash.

Rachel wants to lie in the grass.
Jacko feeds her toasted pecans.

Tasting the arsenic of the red flesh
she spits and feels to relieve herself.

Leah giggles. Jacko is blind. Reaches across.
Touches darkness, soft darkness. Feels a cool sweaty

neck, then a trail of beads down to mud forever,
while Rachel retches against a live oak tree.

They couple quickly like a dream,
Leah patting his clumsy back like a baby.

Rachel's sobs carry like breathing,
then stop. Here in Al's dream yard,

the light is turning, the pink of holy morning.
Seven more years of lost labour, waiting for heaven,

Jacko Jacobus squanders his cherished dream:
Rachel, the soft-eyed one, waiting for his touch.

Leah feels her womb awake
to the coming of seed.

RETURN

for Kamau Brathwaite

This is the path to new life and to death,
  renaming the earth with familiar sounds,

calling, calling across the green hills
  in three-part harmony, everything jumping,

the way the snare springs you back,
  what to do but jump to the pumping sound.

This is the path by the river, now red,
  now reeking of stale bauxite,

the fish are dead, the shrimp are dead,
  the sea snake dead, the algae dead.

This is the path of new music that calls
  Africa, calls it without knowing,

the pattern of the drums on the skin.
  This is the way the snare makes you jump.

My heart beats like a baby's, alert each time
  I embrace dark nights alone.

Here in the stillness, waiting for the crack
  of something, my head pulses in fear.

Then I look for open fields away from predator
  gunman, a place to wet my body in night dew.

I have returned to plant new grass, new trees,
  and now I know I have returned knowing only

that when death comes, I will be ready,
  for home fires flame in my tender heart, my heart.

TRAVELLER

Things have not changed much.
  The treeline is almost the same.

This journey over oceans was long
  and we jettisoned much on the way,

but our eyes were not startled by the new
  light, and the earth still took to our feet.

At night I would dream it was simply
  another long march, a long trek from the disease

of the river-fly to another space, another landscape.
  Once, we walked for months, till we came to a dry place

where the earth was orange, flaming orange and dusty;
  we had never seen anything like this before.

Still, we buried our dead in the sand,
  and at night around the fire and drums

the ancestors found their way to our feet,
  to our hearts, to our livid tongues.

So this is all familiar as yesterday,
  and the yams grow large in this soil,

and my fingers still cake with the dirt,
  making tradition in new land, new spaces,

and in the sky, Nyankopon looks on
  with the same unwinking eye of the moon.

HOW THE WEDDING LAUGHED

In the red dirt of St. Elizabeth
a pig was slaughtered and a goat,

a pit dug deep and filled with coals
to roast the sow, to roast the goat.

And how the wedding laughed.
The virgins, jealous in their Sunday best,

compared their breasts and hips
with Leah's proud strut and grin,

and how the wedding laughed.
The rum flowed through the night,

the pot of curried goat had no bottom,
and feast, they feasted till daylight came;

yes, how the wedding laughed.
And Leah let her lips be kissed

by an old boyfriend, a cop,
giddy with the sight of her vulnerable white,

her ebony skin all slick with sweat,
her eyes all wet with the stir of rum.

Her lips parted and she bit his tongue
and the people giggled and whispered;

yes, how the wedding laughed.
But Jacko, indulgent, smiled it off

and drank some more, and more, and more
then fell on Rachel's breasts in tears.

Man, how the wedding laughed!
Yes, how the wedding laughed!

LONGING

Reading the yellowing leaves of scripture,
  cocooned in the soft quiet of night,

Rachel dreams of love, its treachery
  like the terrible warmth of stolen embraces.

Rachel sees Jacko, bandy-legged and tough,
  kicking stones on the marl road,

waiting for the bossman, foreman to come
  in his red pick-up with promise of work.

Rachel sees Jacko dragging a slaughtered predator crow
  from the edge of the ponds of rainbow trout,

while its mates circle in the blue beyond and wait
  to scatter the flies from the drying blood.

In this she sees the written hand of God
  guiding her in her quiet time of revelations.

Rachel sees Jacko making his seed froth,
  planting it in shallow soil, and gloating Leah

pat-patting his back, the smell of light
  perfume and Limacol in the air.

Rachel prays the prayer of impossible love:
  of fate, of God's wisdom, dead wives, lonely widowers,

comforting Jacko Jacobus in his grief –
  all this in the scriptures like prophecy in the wind.

BIRTHING ROOM

There is much white in the birthing room,
the purest light from the brilliant day.

She had stood and finished the stew peas and rice
and walked in the sun through bright contractions.

Now propped like a queen on cushions of white
Leah's crown of unruly hair spreads like water.

The midwife, starched to severe purity,
commands the ritual of birthing

with silver and bright steel instruments,
prodding, feeling, squeezing, looking.

Push... now... push... now... push... Wait.
Push... yuh not breathing, chile... Bear down! Wait!

And Leah floats in a cloud of
white pain until the howl shatters

the coming down of everything wet,
everything flowing river-wet, down.

The boy is swaddled in white
and named softly, named for a mountain.

His eyes tight, conceal the blade of his future,
the blood red of so much blood shed by his hand.

But quiet is the light on this bright
day when babies are soft as cotton.

Leah dreams of clouds and clouds
swimming in the brilliance of blue.

Even at night, laid out as in a coffin,
   he can't sleep for the evil in his heart;

he is weaving baskets to catch fish
   swimming home in fish water;

that is the sinfulness of the wicked;
   and his wife does not know

why he turns and turns all night,
   mouth muttering as if there are pebbles in his heart.

There is an oracle in my heart
   tells me to speak like this;

but I am not a prophet, just a player
   of songs, a lyrics man, with two sacs

of blessed seed to spawn a generation
   of miracle-makers. My task is just to plow the earth,

plant my seed and then, like some ephemeral
   insect, become one with the mist.

But I know the wicked man and his works,
   know his cunning machinations that seem

so gloriously brilliant in their diabolic wit
   here in the light of day. But who would

guess the planning he does deep in the night
   tossing on the fetid damp of his sepulchral sheets?

For a thirsting man caught here, stranded
  late at night between two dry hills,

to have my prayers answered is to taste sweet water,
  and the passing of fear – fear of the drawn gun

ready to spill my simple brains
  on this cooking tarmac; fear of the old ghosts

rising from the sea with their unknowable
  anger, ready to strike me dumb, dry my seed –

the passing of such fears brings cool calm breezes
  to my soul, and I know that the sound

of gigantic wings flapping is
  a sign of the love of heaven.

Few songs but these tried and proven
  hymnals of majestic patience can

sing the largeness of my gratitude
  in these dark times. Continue your wash

of love for my seed and their seed;
  bring stones to crush the blundering heads

of my enemies, and may the heart of the sweating,
  evil man, seeping all that pig flesh,

stop so sudden with startle and dread,
  never to start again, never to start again.

LION HEART

Showing love under the soft lamplight,
  cradling his slumbering head in her thighs,

Rachel uses her sensitive soft fingertips
  to find the roundness of ripe pimples,

squeezing lines of pale yellow,
  sweet satisfaction of popped bumps.

And even after all oil and matter
  has been drawn out, she caresses

the slack face of Jacko Jacobus,
  putting dreams into his lidded eyes,

putting love into the rugged curve
  of his lump of nose, the roughness of his chin,

the severe scars of his broken lips,
  the stone of his tight leather forehead;

like feeling the shape of the found skull
  of some long forgotten ancestor.

Showing love like this,
  she sings soft, *fi mi love 'ave lion heart...*

COVENANT

for Michelle

Stone in water,
  pile the stones.

Stone in my heart,
  heart is water.

There is a pillar where we stopped
  and found love by a stream,

where we drank sweetly and rested
  while the sun washed the tree tops.

Pillar of our journey, smooth flat stones
  taken from the cool of streams.

This is the promise of our many journeys,
  hands clasped, faces looking away.

My island is a monument of love;
  stone is water, jam-rock is the promised

hope of these dark times, my love,
  but I feel your water caressing stone

and I am washed, washed by your
  love, stone in water on this island

green with the long caress of
  water on the constant stone.

My heart is water
  heart of stone, always adamant.

TRICKSTER

Every trick executed with that flick of my wrist,
every deft sleight of hand by me, Jacobus,

was a way to prepare the language of my path,
a way to tell how I would be met on the road.

My way was made by a winking of the eye,
for my way was perilous and the rocks were large;

and though I know that I made my bed of woes,
there was an urge to live beyond the moment,

to survive the onslaught of time's wrath,
to make it to the other side, intact, if

somewhat tarnished by the journey.
This tracing of my many journeys,

stretches out like delicate parchment.
The roads are strewn with piles of stones

for each successful trick, each quick
foot-shuffle, working my magic like that.

And God is my light and salvation,
not because of the purity of my soul,

(that was too long ago, and besides,
I was too young to take credit for it),

but because of the prophecy of his own mouth.
Beyond me, beyond my ways, beyond it all,

there is an inexorable end he has made,
warts, deceptions, slow tongues, lies, and all.

This was the path made before me:
I bore seed to make nations tremble,

me, unworthy trickster, with too little faith
to depend on the miracle of God – I, Jacobus

made my own paths, and now swallow the bitter weed
of my fallen ways. It is faithlessness, but it is so

when you have been called to this walk of destiny;
it is all you can do to remain awake

for the fanfare and the tributes at the end of the way,
it is all you can do to be human again, it is all.

FAITH

Every creator is a trickster.
  Every progenitor is a wit-man.

Grey like this, I look dull;
  it has been a long, long time

since my faithless hurtle into adventure,
  making this history of impossible progeny,

making the sky explode in blue and white,
  with silken scatterings of delicate lines

like the broken strings of stitched flesh.
  It was I who made that sky expand to bursting;

this is what I believed in my faithless heart,
  but that was a long time ago, and besides,

the folks are all dead,
  and the earth has moved on.

Now grey and faithful, I watch for the coming of rain
  in season, in time; for the coming of Sahara sands

on the belly of the Atlantic winds, in season,
  in time – these miracles; I watch with knowing

boredom spinning leaves, for this is the way of the Lord,
  this predictable calm of each new morning,

this is the way of the Lord. I watch the slowing
  of my bones, the collapsing of my blackening lungs,

the dying of my memory – these things I know
  to be the way of the Lord, the way of my journey

to that heaven of blue and streaks of white,
  the boredom of faithfulness, nothing left

for the wizardry of my wit, as I watch the leaves
  shed themselves and fall, falling down,

as I watch my daughters multiply themselves,
  my sons wreak havoc on the nations.

There is nothing new in the will of the Almighty;
  with faith all things are painfully possible,

with faith all things must be.
  Then I will lie and rest my bones,

retired trickster, joker, magic-maker,
  retired into the quiet of belief in mornings.

BLESSED

The blessing of God is an intangible
as trustworthy as myth – a new day in the clamour

of traffic, smoke and the acrid remnants
of stray dogs burning on tyres; the blessing

of God is an intangible, a truth spoken
but fleeting, like the sun sucks up dew.

Still the dreams come at night:
the possessed journeys into impossible light

at sea bottom, where among bones and shells
the truth of ancestral angst is rekindled;

nights galloping the unruly land, a horse
bearing the driving lash of the spirit, the drum;

the limping elder with his walking stick;
the half-man, half-insect spinning webs;

the ladder to the earth from the sky
carrying messages as old as creation.

He wakes with the voice of prophecy
washing his body, his seed, his future.

The judgment is simple:
Your righteousness shall not save you, deceiver,

but the stale brittle of your moistureless soul
will flame into a light for the nations.

Thus saith the Lord of hosts.
All in dreams, these intangibles of life.

HIS PRESENCE

The presence of God is like a flame
  melting the wax beneath it,

like the feet of the wind
  pounding the mountains to rubble,

like floodwater
  flowing down the slopes,

like the white devouring of glaciers
  through the green of river valleys,

like the precise incisions
  of hill rice growers

shaping generations of steps
  on the mountainsides.

This is the presence of the Lord;
  thanks be to God.

poems from

REQUIEM

RESEARCH

... for me that was New York City, that was where the pain was.

Tom Feeling,

You did not have to imagine
the masks of agony,
did not have to research
the eyes' blank stare,

Did not have to study ethnic tribes
to see the shape of Africa
in the lips and noses
the weight of buttocks,

Did not have to invent
the blues of suffering,
the jazz of rebellion,
the fire of survival,

'Cause you looked across
Brooklyn and saw the road-weary
gaze of them who still travel
in the belly of ships,

Them who still sit among the cinder,
the soot, riding that freedom train
to the factories of the North
herded into the tombs of the ghetto;

Stared at your face in the mirror
after the stomach unfurls,
the skin smarting from being

spat on, shat on, pissed on.
You draw lines from somewhere cherished;
our gasps, groans, whispers
are the minor-keyed, antiphonal melodies
of our recognition of self.

We enter your holocaust
with trepidation and leave the stench
with tears, and something like gratitude
for the waters of healing, the salt, the light.

BIRD FLIES

bird flies

I have not known peace,
not known mornings
like bird flight.

I have not woken
to a shrine
ancient as my skin,
to the scent of offered blood.

I search my memory
for icons of remembrance;
coke bottles, washboards,
nets woven in raked soil
for new grass, my signs.

I have dreamt
of something beyond
the clamour of this city,
dreamt of robust youth
sprinting through the savannah.

bird flies

I have not known peace,
not known mornings
like bird flight.

There is a soft saxophone
choking on its own sound,
making like a bird in flight
when you close your eyes.

Open them to see the whites
of a Black man's eyes

searching you for something
lost, blowing in sharp
bursts from his tender
lips, white eyes chained
to the trembling glass
of rot-gut, no ice —

bird flies

I have not known peace,
not known mornings
like bird flight;
no one's flying these days.

CRIME OF PASSION

The baobab tree, implacable witness,
to the smashing of what little we had,
does not offer shelter. I inscribe

these revelations in words that search
for a song in the faceless shadows
of the men who string my ankles,

drag me here. Oh to stay in the simple
dialectic of hatred and brutality
there at the edge of my flaming hut,

to remain in that fire-bright place
of purest hate, the stranger, a beast,
my fist clear-eyed, pounding life

from his faceless howls. All this long before
the gospel of crosses, blood; the song
of promised lands I have embraced,

long before I copulated
with his books and gave birth to words,
long before he found my tongue,

could sing with my tongue, owned my tongue
while I toyed with his. Now my fist
is a cataracted beast, unable to shake

the monkey of affinity from my back.
Neurotic me, when once all was simple
passion, now I cannot kill without premeditation,

cannot act without the legacy of that baobab
staring mutely at the ravage of my hut
before time, before time, before time.

REQUIEM

I sing requiem
for the dead, caught in that
mercantilistic madness.

We have not built lasting
monuments of severe stone
facing the sea, the watery tomb,

so I call these songs
shrines of remembrance
where faithful descendants

may stand and watch the smoke
curl into the sky
in memory of those

devoured by the cold Atlantic.
In every blues I hear
riding the dank swamp

I see the bones
picked clean in the belly
of the implacable sea.

Do not tell me
it is not right to lament,
do not tell me it is tired.

If we don't, who will
recall in requiem
the scattering of my tribe?
In every reggae chant

stepping proud against Babylon
I hear a blue note

of lament, sweet requiem
for the countless dead,
skanking feet among shell,

coral, rainbow adze,
webbed feet, making as if
to lift, soar, fly into new days.

VULTURES

Companions of our march,
vultures can smell
the sour of death.

All instinct,
there is a simple patience
in their watch. Fallen,

the body still breathes.
Out of the corner of the eye
the slipping soul can see

the flutter of vultures
calmly waiting for the twitch
to slow to a smoothness.

They hop forward with each gasp,
circle, respecting the light of life
in the eye, then, quietly, they feast.

There is no other way back
to the kraal except by the giving
of final breath; death comes and then flight.

What is left is mere grotesquery;
but the vultures understand the simple
equations of ecology; theology eludes them.

Circling above, they track the lines,
footprints like train tracks,
that fade with the whipped wind.

These vultures speckle a blue sky
and learn the trade routes
to the castles by the sea;

they arrive, bloated, low-bellied
like Russian cargo planes,
and rest in the yard, sentinels

to this trade in carrion,
this scavenging of flesh,
this transporting of limbs.

They follow the thin trail
of the ship's cut, still smelling
the canker of a slaver,

but falter as the salt grows tart,
and the smell of earth dries up.
They can return to old haunts.

After a final circle
they fade into the horizon.
The ship slouches on.

CAVE

Above us is granite,
below us the give of wood
seasoned with constant blood,
piss, shit, vomit, sweat —
our essence seeping out of us.

We left our souls behind
in that last light of the courtyard
where two children stood
crying without tears.

We watched, as one, the way
our souls lifted with the stench
of our fear, trying to catch the current
back to the ancient shrine.

The children howled,
wooden shackles tethering them,
their nakedness a smudge
on the pale white of limestone.

We crawled, soulless, but with the suggestion
of song into our tomb. Beyond this is burial
repeated in ritual efficiency:
the cave, the hull, the strange ocean.

Sometimes in the blues
you sense a dry, hollow cry;
it is the wail from the granite cave
caught in mid-flight, mid-flight.

CROSS

At the helm of the boat
a cross to light them home.

Gail is gobbled by the lounge chair,
incongruous black softness in my office.
She gazes at the strewn pictures,
mute images of callous ways,
and calls herself a "Generation X"
who doesn't give a hoot what they want
to call her, 'cause she cares
but doesn't have to march to care.

She mutters at the open page,
"Their backs must have hurt.
For days, no movement; it would kill me."

At the helm of the boat,
parting the undulating sheets of white,
a cross to light them home.

"How could they go for months
like that, like that, like that?"

At the helm of the boat,
the ghost man counts the beat
of the oars' dip and rise
in the fluent Atlantic,
heading towards the tapestry
of ropes, masts, canvas –
the uneasy cutter waiting
against a muddy sky

a cross to light them home

"Amazing grace how sweet the sound..."

HATE

for Joseph Cinque and the Africans on the Amistad

I understand hate.
I used to know fear.

That flame in my eyes
Not madness, nothing so benign.

Just pure hate.
I could eat your heart   raw.

SHAME

If I heard the wail of a child,
over the lap of the sea,
heard the ebb of its whimpering,
eyes searching the void
for the familiar dark
of my face, my womb would burst,
my throat would open
and shatter the sky
with its scream.

They stand him
on wooden planks
to stare at the gawking heads
of men, too defiant
to make the passage to nowhere.
He stares, eyes tearing from the salt
in the humid air.
He must not hear me
stifling my moans,
numbing my flesh
from the stabbing
of those bloody penises

At night
the creaking of the boat
lulls the tomb
and the babies,
chests weary with howling,
moan in reverie
while we lick our wounds,
wipe the wet from our thighs,
avert our gaze from the shame
of men, still alive, now boys,
witnesses to our abuse.

BURIAL AT SEA

The vultures of the seas
can smell the drip
of ebbing life
seeping through
the cracks in the wood.

It is morning;
before the hot of midday,
the ghosts walk through
unshackling the dead,
lifting the leather and bones.

No words spoken,
no libation,
just a ritual tossing
of bodies overboard,
the captain pricking his ledger.

Lloyd's will give sterling
for jettisoned cargo.
To round up the numbers
the whimpering sickly
are tossed into the ribbons of foam.

Now I can stretch my legs
my feet feel blood again;
the dead leave space
for the living.
The ancestors have forgotten us.

WARRIOR

i

Like a whip
unfurled,
his body
still taut
from sprinting
behind the fleeing elephant
gathers the ghost
and with a sudden plunge
guts the monster.
There is blood,
and the smell of bile.
The warrior
laughs, staring at the blood.
There is shock in his eyes
when they bring him down

ii

Only to hoist
him up

iii

Jerking,
jerking,
then still,
life is breathed out,
he dangles,
the warrior,
from the mast.

Before you look
you smell
the swelling flesh;
the salt makes leather
of his skin;
flies nurtured
in the meat
mask the white
of his eyes.

You think
the rotting
will cause the neck
to give, but the skin
is now leather;
the rope
finds the grooves
of the spine,
hooks in.

I see the thong
of his member
wither;
it falls.
The ghost

stares at the shrunken snake
as if staring at his own
manhood. Somebody laughs.

vii

It is hard now
to smell the canker.
The wind blows through
him like a flag.
The body is gutted
by the turning gulls.

The watch cries
Land!

viii

I leave my heart
with the dangling warrior

I leave my heart
with the dangling warrior.

His teeth grin back
at me.

RAT

This belly of the ship
is a tomb.

The rats clear the bones;
the skin dries.

They have forgotten
the curled-up body

of a baby long dead.
I cannot smell him,

I can only hear
the scratching of rats

dragging his bones
into their holes.

The rats never grow thin,
beasts in the belly of the whale.

LAND HO

I cannot speak the languages
spoken in that vessel,
cannot read the beads
promising salvation.

I know this only,
that when the green of land
appeared like light
after the horror of this crossing,

we straightened our backs
and faced the simplicity
of new days with flame.
I know I have the blood of survivors

coursing through my veins;
I know the lament of our loss
must warm us again and again
down in the belly of the whale,

here in the belly of this whale
where we are still searching for homes.
We sing laments so old, so true,
then straighten our backs again.

poems from

SHOOK FOIL

SOME TENTATIVE DEFINITIONS I

'Lickle more drums...'
Bob Marley

First the snare crack,
a tight-head snare crack like steel,
rattle, then cut, snap,
crack sharp and ring at the tail;
calling in a mellow mood,
with the bass, a looping lanky
dread, sloping like a lean-to,
defying gravity and still limping
to a natural half-beat riddim,
on this rain-slick avenue.

Sounds come in waves
like giddy party types
bringing their own style and fashion,
their own stout and rum,
their own Irish Moss
to this ram jam session.

Everything get like water now
the way steady hands
curve round a sweat-smooth waistline,
guiding the rub, the dub, so ready.
This sound is Rock Steady
syrup slow melancholy,
the way the guitar tickling
a bedrock drum and bass,
shimmering light over miry clay.

LIGHT LIKE A FEATHER, HEAVY AS LEAD

Bob Marley, 'Misty Morning'

All green light seeping into the morning
the smell of coconut oil and ackee,
lazy reggae pulsing through the thin boards.
This sleeping Sunday morning,
the hymns of the Pentecostal church
tucked into the dense green of August Town
swim like prophecy in waves
threading through the faint drum and bass
of the transistor chatting upstairs.

I hear Marley's thinning voice
cut after cut until I ache
from the apprentice cicatrices,
ears now alert to the gravel thin wail
of the original shortass reggae organizer
dubbing me bloody truths from the thin
concentric grooves – round and round
maddening gyre of prophecies,
spiralling mysteries and no clue,
no vision of some monumental journey
over strewn palm fronds and the praise of believers
through holy Kingston – the prophet slips by unnoticed;
(Jamaicans have never understood the hysteria
of Beatlemania, we die, not for pop icons,
but for sweet-mouthed politicians, we die).
This black, glowing vinyl of trapped sound
is all that is left, all that is left
of the rhygin, word-weaving prophet.

My fingers stretch and flow through
the whisper of old revelations like mist,
the rough of the cracked snare and one drop

sound is washed by something of a dream,
I cannot find my way through the smoke.
It is hours before a long-time-coming
sea breeze, still warm from its journeys,
tickles the morning; everything giggles,
everything is light as mute anomie,
while she closes his stiff eyes.

PISGAH

Til from Mount Pisgah's lofty heights,
I'll lift my wing and take my flight...

I did not know this then, since the sound
reminded me of life stirring at the bottom
of the sea, glinting fish, flaming coral
all flashes of energy coming like the lock-step
of a rhythm-section getting it right and tight;
gummy as beach heat and the smell of fish;
a mad man dancing to oblivion in Half Way Tree.
A way of making it all livable.
Since the sound was life-making,
I did not know it was a dirge,
a lamenting anthem to the Natty Dread's
unmoored spirit making its final journey:

passing down First Street
then skipping on to Second Street,
skanking through to Third Street,
wailing a prayer on Fourth Street,
lighting up souls on Fifth Street,
talking to two dread on Sixth Street
trying to reach, want to reach
gotta reach the Seventh Street
cause somewhere there is heaven street;
owning every crack in the concrete,
loving every scraggly stunted tree,
naming the dry ghetto beachhead,
a mystical place of cremated souls;
he dances the streets of Trenchtown
re-loving the path of survival, Natty Dread!

Then like wind he makes his last swooping pass,
sea winds fingering guitar strings,
then gone, then gone, then gone, then gone.

I AM A STRANGER ON EARTH

I'm alone in the wilderness, I'm alone...

Culture

i

There are days when this unfamiliar earth
  speaks to me and calls me
stranger, alien, brief sojourner here.
  It comes with the discovery of a new flower
the name of which I study with devotion and awe;
  or the way a sudden storm whips
the fallen leaves and bends the trees.
  I stand in the mind of the storm,
I feel like an obstruction – dispensable.
  The earth never tells me my true home.
I have never seen it, not even in dreams;
  I have no assurances that it is there.
I sit among stones and dried bramble
  and feed on the mysteries I can find
taking shape after the rain of tongues
  from the congregation gathered outdoors
to meet the light of sun, like white sheets
  put out to bleach on zinc in the blaze.
Here, I tighten my eyes to block out the dizzy
  distraction of spinning leaves,
of these strange flowers bursting about me.

ii

Sometimes, when the head is giddy,
when the body finds its pulse,
  when the read word becomes an incantation
of light, like a rightly deciphered poem,
  I see faces of my enemies,
the arrogant and proud builders of snares,
  wincing at the swoop of vengeance; a sword

falling, falling on them, upon them.
   Grown men weep and grovel for mercy
as the sword descends. I feel no remorse
   since this carnage is of another life
I do not know or understand. Besides, the wrath
   of the Almighty, so tutored
in the stench of bloated flesh,
   the quick expiration of last breaths
before his stony stare, is,
   as they say, his business,
and for us, all there is
   is trying. The spilling of blood
leaves me drained and tender
   like the soft place of a lanced boil.

                           iii

   I stir from my trance hungry and thirsty,
and as sudden as a prayer formed, the sky is ashen-
   heavy, sputtering pellets of rain.
I stand before the language of this storm
   again an alien, a sojourner, waiting for a clue
to lead me homeward – a place of quiet rest.
   I know there is a truth in the storm,
but I do not delight in truth; I tremble
   for truth will shackle me
to this unfamiliar earth where guilt, regret,
   remorse for the blood drying in my nails,
must mark my waking moments. I have become comfortable
   as an alien at heart, free of the tyranny
of truth. In this rootless state my poems
   like prayers follow no prescribed path,
but record the slaughter of the wicked
   with cool remove. I embrace my fate
while the wind and water spin about my head.

RUMOUR

My brother, my brother,
my dearly beloved brother...
is dead...

Culture

Who knew, who knew if the news
of his shedding locks in clumps,
his frailer body, his hollow eyes;
who knew, who knew if the news
of a dread gone to pot
was nothing but Babylon lies, lies
like the street telegraph would say,
like the sisters and brothers
labouring their salty way through
Kingston's dry rot would whisper:

Is murder Babylon a try murder the dread;
how a man must live so far from home,
far from yard, with all that stinking smell
of atomic energy and debauchery,
all that sodomy and crack like a curse?
Is murder Babylon a try murder the dread.

Who knew, who knew if the news
was lies to obscure another plot
dem a plot to kill another prophet;
and being so far away, across a phlegmatic,
unfeeling sea, what else to do but
stand aside and watch the fading dread?
Who among us did not believe that some
resurrection song would spring
from his scarred soul and fly
from the ash of a black toe
with him prancing around, wild,

177

guitar swinging like an uzi at the ready,
ready to make an arch of red in the black night,
like Anancy the come-again artist:
lick im kill im, im bounce right back...?

Tuff Gong cyaan dead!

Who dead? Bob dead? How dead? Long dead.

She was not, so the story goes, the same
  after the rape; her body withered
from her lover's touch. Soon her eyes shifted
  from his gaze. She called their love
a worthless thing – vanity, really,
  as her soul found life in deepest prayer;
everything else became a worthless thing.
  She dumped him in the prayer circle,
declaring before God and the elect,
  the futility of their vain tears,
trying to patch the tatters of an old love –
  a worthless thing before the light of faith;
a piece of scrap wood fit for the flame,
  the licking flame of praise.
So she danced before the Lord,
  sweating out the madness of old memories,
the hurt of her assailant's jabbing.
  She cursed the demon,
her nightly guest, the sweat-slick
  visage of the broken-toothed one
panting out his venom until the silence
  of his spent breathing filled the night.
Then like the rush of water into barren places,
  her voice surged, a wail bearing everything
youthful and giddy in her soul, everything
  of the light and cartwheel of unstoppable laughter,
leaving her cold with the wisdom of years,
  sprinkled with specks of time's dust.
Everything now is worthless, she says,
  everything but the word in season,
the devotion of the self to prayer and fasting.
  Here among the ruins of old love,

she walks on hot granite stones without feeling
the heat or the sharp adze nudging her
callous soles. Her journey is one of naming:
naming worthless things rightly
is a gift of holiness, a holy gift of God.

THE INTANGIBLES OF FAITH

Every act of faith is a carefully drafted contract:
  a deal with the eternal.
Feed me with words and I will speak for you.
  The perks, the intangibles
like the smiling accolades of those who hear these words,
  the awe of the heathen at my wit,
these intangibles do not, must not figure in the deal;
  they simply clutter transactions.
But each act of faith is a drafted contract.
  Heal me, and I will walk
the deadly path of ghetto streets offering salvation
  to the gunman and the thief.
I cleanse my head of the brawta I am sure will come
  with the deals I make with the almighty.
I wear a poker face while I offer up my blessings,
  and when the gifts arrive from you,
I accept in hoots of triumph of rejoicing,
  before I crawl to the quiet of my safe
and count the intangibles, uncountable blessings of faith.

SOME TENTATIVE DEFINITIONS VI

'...let me tell you what I know.'

Bob Marley

Police Officer's Club
on Hope Road,
on a wet night,
the teenagers
are turning adult
to the sticky sounds
of Mellow Canary.

I am standing on the edge
smelling too high
of Brut, my silk shirt
already wet with the steam,
hoping she will come
through the croton hedge
like she said she would.

She smiles, calling me
over to the pitch black
of 'Bend Down Low',
and this upright girl
draws me down
so she can tell me
something wet
she knows,
so low,
didn't know
she could ride
so low.

SOME TENTATIVE DEFINITIONS VII

'...I get to understand yuh been livin' in sin'
Bob Marley, 'Bend Down Low'

My fifteen year old
ratchet body
welds itself
to her softer front
and I smell Charlie
mingling with the
chemicals in her hair,
and the rest is a song.

Gyrations of heat,
feet not moving
waistlines going,
trying to find
the groove of sweetest
friction, rolling, rolling,
holding on for dear life
like a buoy on a rocking
sea, like a boat
taken out too far from shore.

In my ears her voice
singing: *Row, fisherman, row*

SHOOK FOIL

i

The whole earth is filled with the love of God.
   In the backwoods, the green light
is startled by blossoming white petals,
   soft pathways for the praying bird
dipping into the nectar, darting in starts
   among the tangle of bush and trees.
My giddy walk through this speckled grotto
   is drunk with the slow mugginess
of a reggae bass line, finding its melody
   in the mellow of the soft earth's breath.
I find the narrow stream like a dog sniffing,
   and dip my sweaty feet in the cool.
While sitting in this womb of space
   the salad romantic in me constructs
a poem. This is all I can muster
   before the clatter of school-children
searching for the crooks of guava branches
   startles all with their expletives and howls;
the trailing snot-faced child wailing perpetual –
   with ritual pauses for breath and pity.
In their wake I find the silver innards of discarded
   cigarette boxes, the anemic pale of tossed
condoms, the smashed brown sparkle of Red Stripe
   bottles, a melange of bones and rotting fruit,
there in the sudden white light of noon.

How quickly the grandeur fades into a poem,
how easily everything of reverie starts to crumble.
    I walk from the stream. Within seconds
sweat soaks my neck and back, stones clog my shoes,
    flies prick my flaming face and ears;
bramble draws thin lines of blood on my arms.
    There is a surfeit of love hidden here;
at least this is the way faith asserts itself.
    I emerge from the valley of contradictions,
my heart beating with the effort, and stand looking
    over the banking, far into Kingston Harbour
and the blue into grey of the Caribbean Sea.
    I dream up a conceit for this journey
and with remarkable snugness it fits;
    this reggae sound: the bluesy mellow
of a stroll on soft, fecund earth, battling the crack
    of the cross stick; the scratch of guitar,
the electronic manipulation of digital sound,
    and the plaintive wail of the grating voice.
With my eyes closed, I am drunk with the mellow,
    swimming, swimming among the green of better days;
and I rise from the pool of sound, slippery with
    the warm cling of music on my skin,
and enter the drier staleness of the road
    that leads to the waiting city of fluorescent lights.

PRAYER FOR MY SON

for Keli

i

When the moist sores sucked strength from your
   frail limbs, I cried out.
Healing came in gradual waves and then you smiled.
   Still, I lie with my silence,
no testimony on my lips, no rejoicing,
   no credit given. I lie.
And there are the days
   of waiting for the wrath to fall,
my punishment for ingratitude,
   collecting miracles like a blooming tree
collects birds, but hides the blossoms
   in skirts of modest green.
Trees have shrivelled for less.
   It is written.
This is the quicksand of Babylon,
   dwelling in this place of stagnant logic.
I find even the magic of poems to be forced.
   I live and eat with a people
of calculating guile, who can't see the light
   of a jewelled night for the orange
glow of fluorescent bulbs. When I testify
   in their midst, they fidget
at the gaucheness of my passion, then adroitly
   make humour and little of my faith.

These days I barely hear my supplicant moan
    under cover of my dreams.
When morning comes, I quickly forget,
    for how can I expect the magic
of healing when my tongue will not
    speak it, proclaim it, herald it?
I wait for the fire to burn the chafe
    as I watch my child's limbs heal.
It is all I can muster in this barren
    place. My last cry will be
a plea for the unfurling of my tongue
    to draw new paths
in this land of the mute and doubting.
    My last prayer spoken,
I wait for the bright miracle to flame
    in the twilight of peace,
between night and morning, when dew
    is lavender scented and cool,
when the sky is russet soft
    with bated hope.

SOME TENTATIVE DEFINITIONS XI

Every time I hear the sound of the whip...

Bob Marley, 'Catch A Fire'

For every *chekeh* of the guitar,
a whip cracks.
How can you hear the sound
and not weep?

Follow the pattern with me,
always on the off.
We are forever searching for spaces
to fill with us.

If you walk straight down on the one,
you will stumble,
cause the reggae walk is a bop
to the off-beat.

We are always finding spaces
in the old scores
to build our homes, temples and dreams,
and we call it back-o-wall.

For every *wooku* of the Hammond B
a body hums.
How can you smell the sound
and still sleep?

BEFORE THE POEM

i

Some things must be left to the logic of the divine;
    if a word declares a path, it is not
our affair to swing machetes, making our own way;
    it is for us only to watch to see the road
appear, made clear for us. And then, with home, walk.
    I have stood upon the mountains
gathered like sentinels around Kingston, such
    purple-green clean in the early evening,
caressed by the swift descent of fog
    while birds dip and soar, towards the grey
of coming night. I have stood on these mountains
    and felt the peculiar safety of a path already made,
of a journey already plotted, tested and taken,
    a time removed from the dry heat of the valley. Now, hands raised,
my head like a livid antennae, I feel
    for the coming word, a way of being in these times.

ii

I tell this now only as a way of recording
a place distinct as the end of prayer: that place
    of hope, before the stark reality
of a still sick child waiting for prayer to take.
    It is a sacred place where poem
is nothing but the dance of new light on grass,
    of music tonguing the quiet of Sunday afternoons:
(this is the hint of a poem about to sprout, long before
    the words are gathered and rendered; there is
a place of calm, an essence that is the fore-poem,
    again, and again, and again, unspoken, but shaped).

I cannot make words here, my limbs move
   building pillars of stone for each revelation.
I do not claim to know the logic of this testament,
   the ubiquitous wisdom of a miracle path,
so I stand dwarfed by a grander design, and wait for
   light in this limbo, wait for illumination.

NEW SOUNDS

He brought the slip of black vinyl,
and let spin the light on black.
Reggae enigmatic engulfed the house,
and in his blue mist of shelter
he tapped his feet to the new sound:
the jazz subtle in the horn section,
calling up the spirit of Don Drummond,
calling up the side-riding of old jazz folk,
calling up Africa in the dread's journey,
the confirmed journey of the man poet
travelling from first to second to third,
nondescript Trench Town streets, still home
for this pop icon, rude bwoy, skanking dread.
And this is how Thelonious Monk was usurped
from the all wooden, hand-crafted gramophone
cabinet, how the Duke got schooled by a thug,
how a newer path of earth birthing life
suggested itself in our home – this clean tight reggae,
the I-Threes melodious in their response to his call.

ii

On nights when rum poured golden and sweet
and laughter shook the louvres,
I would be called out in my raggamuffin threads
to skank a magic number to Bob's
rocking reggae sound. And dance,
I would dance, owning this sound, owning
this rasta revolution, my body contorting,
mimicking old moves until the spirit of this pulse
would take root; I would do things I never

thought I could, never dreamt I could,
my face a permanent scowl, my feet cool
on the solid tiles, dancing, dancing.
The applause would shimmer,
and beaming, returned from the sea voyage,
my eyes filled with the souls I have met on the way,
I would withdraw to my cubicle room,
nodding to the sibling cheers,
still sweating, still floating,
still amazed at this new way of walking.
The record would kick into gear again,
and the voices would rise in deep discourse,
proclaiming this rhygin man the total socialist dream –
a voice of the people, from the people;
and regretting that they can't package the thing,
can't sell the thing, can only watch in awe, and dance.

BLACK HEART

i

Of the three, one blackheart man lives,
the one whose finger prophesied death
for the Chinese producer, bloodsucker,
pointed to his death, to a heart attack
crashing him down sudden like that,
right there in his office, the crime scene
where hundreds of dreams have been stolen
with a hastily secured signature,
where many voices have been captured
in the cage of black vinyl for a few pounds.
And one normal afternoon, patties consumed,
soft drink gulped quickly, shirt back wet,
after a spate of belching, one vomiting fit,
the man drop dead like that,
lying there like a poem among the carpet
of forty-fives grinning in the fluorescent light.

ii

Of the three, one blackheart man lives,
the others are buried beneath the grass,
one the rugged quick tongue of the gangster
dread, stepping razor, crusader of lost causes,
underdog with the wit of a survivor,
his black body boasting bruises
from indiscriminate batons of Babylon's lackeys –
and you can bet he never begged, just cursed
nuff claat, and took the broken jaw
like a trophy – this incarnation

of a Soweto toi toi stumper with no discernible
Boer to make a revolution against,
(for isn't this Paradise where the natives
smile too sweetly to be ruthless?)
just the Shitsem like a windmill.
His eyes would twinkle at the impossible of it
and his mind would construct rastological myths,
the antennae on his head picking up songs
from the waves of the sea at Palisadoes
(and the interviewer nodded with sincere indulgence).
This dread, ambushed by his legacy,
gunned down by an irony so blatant it hurts,
gutted by shot after shot, making him step
searching for solid ground and finding nought
but air, before the head popped. It is finished.

iii

Of the three, one blackheart man lives;
the other, the loner, the mystic star-gazer,
the multicoloured coat-wearer, the short explosion,
defied the bullet, but watched
some white man's disease devour his vulnerable
flesh, like treachery, fading, fading
with a whimper against the good night.
The shell could not hold any longer,
crumbled, letting fly his unconquerable soul,
which travelled into mystery and faith;
gone with all the promise,
perhaps because he trusted too much,
perhaps because he embraced too often...

Of the three, one blackheart man lives,
the one who will not fly on the iron bird,
not trusting Babylon's contraptions,
sipping, sipping the incense of Jah
and pumping out second-rate dancehall tunes.
A tarnished star, with dub appeal,
living through the blackness of a curse,
stoking his own flames of mystery.
He will outlive the poem, he will reorganize
the parts of himself and reinvent his image
before he retires an enigma, a reggae geriatric,
an irrelevant dread with only a satchel
of old songs to his name. Blackheart man,
the true duppy conqueror, showing how rude bwoys
grow grey, showing us the sorrowful mortality
of the skanking old man. The others exploded
in the height of their glory, but he will remind us
that all flesh is dust; even the taut drum skin
of the wailing wailer will shrivel too.
It is how it was written, how it has passed
from generation to generation to generation.

RITA

i

I first saw you cooking in the background
of a jumpy camera shot, while the dread
held forth, constructing his facade of enigma,
dodging the barbs and darts of Babylon with code,
and three times he denied you, called you a sister,
like Isaac did to Rebecca, leaving her there,
hanging like that, open season for Ahimalech
and the boys, that is what you were,
a flower tarnished, just a helping sister,
Martha in the kitchen swollen with child.
And who, watching this, would have known
of the nights he would crawl into your carbolic
womb, to become the man-child again,
searching for a father who rode off on his white steed
and never returned, never sent a message?

ii

For years I thought you had lied,
for it was our way to believe the patriarch,
and who would want to declare the coupling
of the downtown dread with the uptown Miss World,
too sweetly ironic, too much of Hollywood
in this sun-drenched, dust-beaten city?
Who would let your black face, weighed by the insult
disturb our reverie? I did not believe the rumours.
So while the nation grumbled and cussed you out,
declared you gold digger and such the like
when he was buried and celebrated in death,
and you published the wedding photos,
the family snapshots of another time;

when you battled like a higgler for rights,
and played every dubious game in the book,
rough-house, slander, ratchet smile and all,
I called it poetic, the justice you received,
for you played the cards right, no bad card drawn
in your hands, as you sat quietly in the back-room
like a nun, bride of Christ and slave to mission.
And when you knew other men
before the tears could dry from our eyes,
and made another child in your fertile womb,
when your garments of silence were replaced
with the garish gold and silver of decadence,
when you entered the studio to play rude girl,
naughty as hell, talking about feeling damned high,
and rolling your backside like a teenager,
I had to smile at the poetic meaning of it all,
for you fasted before this feast,
you played the wife of noble character
eating the bitter fruit of envy
while the dread sought out the light-skinned
beauties, from London, to L.A., King Solomon
multiplying himself among the concubines.

iii

These days I have found a lesson of patience
in your clever ways, a picture of fortitude
despite the tears – you are Jamaican woman,
with the pragmatic walk of a higgler,
offering an open bed for his mind-weary nights,
an ear for his whispered fears and trepidations,
and a bag of sand for a body to be beaten,
slapped up, kicked and abused; you took it all,
like a loan to be paid in full at the right time.

I no longer blame you for the rabid battles
raging over the uneasy grave of the rhygin dread;
for now I know how little we know of those
salad days in a St. Ann's farmer's one-room shack,
where you made love like a stirring pot,
and watched the stars – for they were the only light.
What potions you must have made to tie, tie
your souls together like this! I simply watch
your poetic flight, black sister, reaping fruit
for the mother left abandoned with a fair-skinned child,
for the slave woman who caressed the head
of some married white master, with hopes
of finding favour when the days were ripe,
all who sucked salt and bitter herbs,
all who scratched dust, scavenged for love,
all who drew bad cards; you have
walked the walk well. The pattern is an old one.
I know it now. It's your time now, daughter.
Ride on, natty dread, ride on, my sister, ride on.

HOW CAN A YOUNG MAN KEEP HIS WAY PURE?

i

The path of the young is strewn
  with stones that have fallen
from an ubiquitous sky. A boy stumbles.
  I travel Kingston's sumptuous lanes,
thick with the green of unruly trees
  and the weekday dreaminess of suburban calm,
eyeing the casual sway of a domestic
  gathering clothes from a nylon line.
She smiles my way only slightly,
  then vanishes into the shadow of a mango tree.
My body is alert to the scent of woman,
  to the slow movement of her body;
and giddy with imaginings,
  I stumble hard from staring into the darkness
trying to draw her out – it is lust I feel,
  fourteen years old and weighed down
by the ambiguities of faith and lust:
  how fervent are my prayers of penitence,
how complete my lustful indulgence.
  I am too young now for middle ground,
though I know I will die forever
  if brought down when my mind is swamped
with the precepts of my libido.
  I seek out purer paths.

ii

Few know the canker in my soul.
  I see them see the enigma of a boy,
secret-keeper, a laugh like a wheeze,
  and the mad doggedness to slave
under a stunted breadfruit tree,
  knocking a cricket ball stuffed in a sock,

199

with the monotony of a poet in training,
    kock, kock, kock, kock, kock,
each stroke weighted like words before the paper,
    until sweat gathers in a muddy pool
there at the roots of the tree.
    The reggae in my head is a secret too,
I keep it secure along with my lies.
    I do not know love, I do not know faithful;
I know only lust and the paths it makes.
    My prayers wrestle with me
like a poem taking shape in my head.

iii

    Sometimes I envy those who follow
the fire and brimstone of the preacher's tongue
    and fall in paroxysms of revelation
there at the altar of light, blissful
    in the consistent path to ecstasy
like the tricks of a couple ten years married,
    making orgasms as routine and dependable
as sleep, food, the idle pleasure of sitcoms.
    I envy them the absence of angst.
My eyes will not stay closed for long,
    I want to see the miracle for myself,
and in my faithlessness I scatter the spirit
    to the other end of the earth.
How can a young man keep his way pure?
    Follow the wind's whisper,
until you reach the end of all walking
    and there, in the moment poised over heaven,
weep, there, weep until
    the water of salts has cleansed and bleached
the flame red of your turbulent soul.
    Then fall with the stones, fall with the stones.

SOME TENTATIVE DEFINITIONS XV

play I some music...

Bob Marley, 'Roots Rock Reggae'

The *chekeh* of a guitar lick
is the marshall ordering of the troops,
the high cutting edge of sound,
a stick beating you to get up,
to stand to the call, the call,
to grow a callous on your soft soul
so hard it makes the shedding of blood
painless like river-flow to the sea.
This is the militant perpetual
of reggae, roots reggae.
Now you can find the blood of Babylon
in the sky; and hear your voice,
cutting the clutter of other voices
with an irrepressible brilliant licking,
a stiff tongue rubbing a knife edge:
chekeh, chekeh, chekeh, chekeh.
This is the bright outer garment of reggae
catching the noon day light.
Ride on, people, ride on.

poems from

MIDLAND

INHERITANCE

O Christ, my craft and the long time it is taking!
Derek Walcott

i

In the shade of the sea grape trees the air is tart
with the sweet sour of stewed fruit rotting
about his sandalled feet. His skin,
still Boston pale and preserved with Brahman
devotion by the hawkish woman
who smells cancer in each tropical wind,
is caged in shadows. I know those worn eyes,
their feline gleam, mischief riddled;
his upper lip lined with a thin stripe
of tangerine, the curled up nervousness
of a freshly shaved moustache. He is old
and cared for. He accepts mashed food
though he still has teeth – she insists and love
is about atoning for the guilt
of those goatish years in New England.
A prophet's kind of old. Old like casket-
aged genius. Above, a gull surveys
the island, stiches loops through the sea and sky –
an even horizon, the bias on which
teeters a landscape, this dark loam of tradition
in which seeds split into tender leaves.

ii

The smudge of colours spreads and dries in the sun.
The pulpy paper sucks in the watercolour,
and the cliché of sea and a fresh beach
seems too easy for a poem. He has written
them all, imagined the glitter and clatter
of silver cuirasses, accents of crude

205

Genoese sailors poisoning the air,
the sand feeling for the first the shadow
of flag and plumed helmet – this old story
of arrival that stirred him as a boy,
looking out over the open plains,
as he cluttered the simple island
with the intrigues of blood and heroes,
his grey eyes searching out an ancestry
beyond the broad laughter and breadfruit-
common grunts of the fishermen, pickled
with rum and the *picong* of *kaiso,*
their histories as shallow as the trace
of soil at the beach's edge where crippled
corn bushes have sprouted. That was years ago;
he has now exhausted the jaundiced language
of a broken civilization.
These days he just chips at his epitaph,
a conceit of twilight turning into
bare and bleak nights. He paints, whistling
Sparrow songs while blistering in the sun.

iii

The note pad, though, is not blank. The words start,
thirteen syllables across the page, then seven
before the idea hesitates. These days
he does not need to count, there is in his head
a counter dinging an alarm like the bell
of his old Smith Corona. His line breaks
are tidy dramas of his entrances
and exits, he will howl before the darkness.
This ellipsis is the tease of a thought,
the flirtatious lift of a yellow skirt
showing a brown taut thigh – a song he knows
how to hum but can't recall the lyrics, man –
an airy metaphor – taken up

by a flippant sea breeze going some place
inland, carrying the image, snagged
by the olive dull entanglement
of a thorny patch. At eight he lays
the contents of his canvas book bag
on the sand, organizing the still life
like honed stanzas. He scoops the orange pulp
of papaya, relishing the taste of fruit, this bounty
harvested from the ant-infested fragile tree
that bleeds each time its fruit is plucked.
The flesh is sunny. He knows the fishermen warn
it will cut a man's nature, dry up
his sap; that women feed their men pureed
papaya in tall glasses of rum-punch
to tie them down, beached, benign pirogues
heading nowhere. He dares the toxins
to shrivel him, to punish him
for the chronic genius of crafting poems
from the music of a woman's laugh
while he chews slowly. A poem comes to him
as they sometimes do in the chorus
of a song. It dances about in his head.
He does not move to write it down – it will wait
if it must, and if not, it is probably
an old sliver of long discarded verse.

iv

The old men in the rum shop are comforted
as they watch him limp along the gravel
road, wincing at the sharp prod of stones
in his tender soles, the knees grinding
at each sudden jar – just another ancient
recluse with his easel folded under
his arm, a straw hat, the gull-grey eyes

seeing the sea before he clears the hill.
They know him, proud of the boy – bright as hell
and from good people. There is no shared language
between them, just the babel of rum talk
and cricket sometimes. Under his waters
he talks of Brussels, Florence, barquentines,
Baudelaire, rolling the words around
like a cube of ice – they like to hear
the music he makes with tongue; the way
he tears embracing this green island,
this damned treasure, this shit hole of a treasure.
Sometimes if you don't mind sharp, you would think
him white, too, except for the way him hold
him waters, carry his body into the sun
with the cool, cultivated calm of a rumhead.
Him say home like it come from a book;
hard to recognize when him say home
that is this dry beachhead and tired earth
him talking. They like it, anyway, the way
they like to hear 'Waltzing Matilda' sung
with that broad Baptist harmony to a *cuatro*
plunked, to hear it fill an old song night.

v

If he is my father (there is something
of that fraying dignity, and the way
genius is worn casual and urbane – aging
with grace) he has not lost much over the years.
The cigarette still stings his eyes and the scent
of Old Spice distilled in Gordon's Dry Gin
is familiar here by the sea where a jaunty
shanty, the cry of gulls and the squeak
of the rigging of boats are a right backdrop –
but I have abandoned the thought, the search
for my father in this picture. He's not here,

though I still come to the ritual death watch
like a vulture around a crippled beast,
the flies already bold around its liquid
eyes, too resigned to blink. I have come
for the books, the cured language, the names
of this earth that he has invented,
the stories of a town, and the way
he finds women's slippery parts in the smell
and shape of this island, the making
and unmaking of a city through
the epic cataclysm of fire,
eating the brittle old wood, myths dancing
in the thick smoke like the grey ashen debris
of sacrifice. It is all here with him —
this specimen living out his twilight days,
prodigious as John's horror — the green
uncertain in the half light. When we meet
he is distant, he knows I want to draw
him out, peer in for clues. He will not be drawn out,
he is too weary now. He points his chin
to the rum shop, to an old man, Afolabe,
sitting on the edge of a canoe, black
as consuming night. I can tell
that he carries a new legend in his terrible
soul each morning, a high tower over the sea.

vi

I could claim him easily, make of him
a tale of nurture and benign neglect;
he is alive, still speaks, his brain clicks
with the routine of revelations
that can spawn in me the progeny
of his monumental craft. These colonial
old men, fed on cricket and the tortured

indulgences of white schoolmasters
patrolling the mimic island streets
like gods growing grey and sage-like in the heat
and stench of the Third World; they return
to the reactionary nostalgia
during their last days — it is the manner
of aging, we say, but so sad, so sad.
I could adopt him, dream of blood and assume
the legacy of a divided self.
But it would ring false quickly; after all
my father saw the Niger eating out
a continent's beginnings; its rapid
descent to the Atlantic; he tasted
the sweet *kelewele* of an Akan
welcome, and cried at the uncompromising
flame of *akpetechi*. The blood of his sons
was spilled like libation into the soil, and more:
in nineteen twenty-six, an old midwife
buried his bloodied navel string, and the afterbirth
of his arrival, at the foot of an ancient
cotton tree there on the delta islands
of Calabar. My blood defines the character
of my verse. Still, I pilfer (a much better word),
rummage through the poet's things to find the useful,
how he makes a parrot flame a line
or a cicada scream in wind; the names
he gives the bright berries of an island
in the vernacular of Adam and the tribe.

vii

I carry the weight of your shadow always,
while I pick through your things for the concordance
of your invented icons for this archipelago.
Any announcement of your passing

is premature. So to find my own strength,
I seek out your splendid weaknesses.
Your new poems are free of the bombast
of gaudy garments, I can see the knobs
of your knees scarred by the surgeon's incisions
to siphon water and blood from bone;
I stare at your naked torso – the teats
hairy, the hint of a barreled beauty
beneath the folding skin. I turn away
as from a mirror. I am sipping your blood,
tapping the aged sap of your days while you grow
pale. You are painting on the beach, this is how
the poem began – I am watching you watching
the painting take shape. I have stared long enough
that I can predict your next stroke – your dip
into the palette, your grunts, your contemplative
moments, a poised crane waiting for the right
instance to plunge and make crimson ribbons
on a slow moving river. These islands
give delight, sweet water with berries,
the impossible theologies
of reggae, its metaphysics so right
for the inconstant seasons of sun and muscular
storm – you can hear the shape of a landscape
in the groan of the wind against the breadfruit
fronds. I was jealous when at twenty, I found
a slim volume of poems you had written
before you reached sixteen. It has stitched in me
a strange sense of a lie, as if all this
will be revealed to be dust – as if I learned
to pretend one day, and have yet to be found out.

HOLY DUB

> ...round
> my mud hut I hear again
> the cry of the lost
> swallows, horizons' halloos, found-
> ationless voices, voyages
>
> *Kamau Brathwaite*

i

Let us gather, then, the legend of faith,
truth of our lives in this crude foment of days.

We are so afraid to look to the sky, so cowed, we whisper
of straight paths while a nation grows fat on its own flesh.

Our gospel – our testament – makes martyrs of us.
Another life,
scribbles the scribe, his parchment sucking the blood
of root dyes.

We keep these hymns we've sung through time as stations of our
      journeys.

Come to the waters
There is a vast supply,
There is a river,
That never shall run dry.
Hallelujah!

ii

His afro recedes, creeping towards the nape creaturely,
his forehead is a veined, leathered casing.

The lamplight is guarded by the soot-stained,
wafer-thin glass, with its simple web of doilies

in pale yellow paint – such basic
craft, such splendour in useful things.

He is writing himself into a brittle savannah,
and the mother's calm song he hears is the meaning of faithfulness.

Too-too bobbii
Too-too bobbii.

Her sound carries for miles while her choleric
child fatigues the night with a wailing counterpoint.

The remembrance of old blood makes his skin
accept the sun. The livery is long burnished.

The music of lullabies turns about the poet's head.
His skin has grown darker here – *obroni* black man.

He speaks Ewe, understands the pidgin of mosquitoes.

iii

Between click-filled night and pink dawn,
Beethoven's miserable lament

circles the bungalow that squats beneath the naked
mesh of a *yoyi's* canopy. He finds comfort

in this music, so like the orange dry of the grass lands,
the deep blues of memory. In the symphony's turn

is a thick sweetness of cheap wine and the substance
of fresh bread, still warm, broken by rough hands.

He records the gospel of the desert people,
poor folk whose mornings are oblations to light.

This poet is a *griot* in search of a village. He will forget
all dreams come sunlight. He fears this most.

For decades they will remain myths of a better life,
until he reaches the wilderness of his last dawns,

in a too cold loft over Greenwich Village where he will
try to make verse like they used to make psalms:

to last and last.

LIMINAL

I should have been born in the epoch of flesh
mongering, the time of moral malaise, to hear
the blues crawling from the steaming dungeons
of first blues folk; their lyric moaning
against the encroaching gloom;
I should have heard the iambic ebb and roll
of sea lapping against an alien shore,
the boom of wind in sails, the quick-repeat
auctioneer's scatology, that maddening knocking.
But I've arrived in this other time, waiting
upon an old woman's prayer, to carry the tears and laughter
so long preserved in the tightly knotted hem
of her skirt where she keeps herbs, a broken tooth,
cowrie shells, kola nuts, and the soft lavender
of a wild flower's petals; aged good and strong.
I am gathering the relics of a broken threnody,
lisping psalms — all I have — and crying salt and wet.

SUN STROKES

For Sena

i

My daughter tells me that the sun is a ball of gasses;
that flames are hard to define, but heat she understands:
pressure plus gasses equals heat.
These equations, she explains — she is six this month.

ii

Bonfires around martyrs were merciful — why my daughter
knows this is beyond me.

Wet straw stuffed into the dark cleavages in the bramble
before the execution

caused the smoke to kill — a few coughs, then an airless, painless death
while the muttering

priests repeated Hail Mary's full of grace — my daughter tells me
most of this. A prelude

to an impossible question, I fear. But she has no questions,
she just asks, *Did you know?*

iii

Sometimes I see a bloated head in the sun,
the shape of a boxer's clean-shaven head from behind.
I am seeing paintings the way my daughter does —
finding the poetics of discovery in the things I don't know.

There, see that swath of red paint –
it is a flame frolicking over his crumbling back,
red patterns sending threads of yellow smoke into the blue,
all dancing at the edges of the sun – the gasses, the heat:

Sunspot Maximum.

At the edges everything flakes into a sun-beaten smear of oil
on uncured canvas, the way art rots in the humid tropics.

iv

All that is left is a scream that makes us turn only to be
    blinded by the sun.

Amber threads web our vision's edge with false gold, unreliable
    as the scream we heard.

It was not my daughter, though I thought it was. I imagined it.
    She is sitting there

among open art books, telling stories to herself – a sweet
    calculus of faith.

The refraction of flaming colour from the glossy prints
    catches her skin afire.

No smoke here, just the pure embrace of flame and light as her hands
    run over the soft

paper blue skies. She explains that mystery too: the blue of skies;
    then she's whole again.

MAP MAKER

After Fenwick

...As I was saying – is so bush work stay. Especially on a job like this... Just bide your time. Another couple morning, the survey done, you pack you bag and home, Canje cobweb left behind.

Wilson Harris

i

In a tinder-box frame, the light leaks
through gaps in the rotting panels
and salt air from the sea and brackish river
softens the collected folders until they green and bleed
into the wood, returning to the roaches,
to the smell of worms, to the earth, to the tick of parasites.

An old man with glassed eyes and skin
like the insides of a tangerine peel, guides me
through the shelves to the dank corner smelling
of jungle funk so thick it lingers like the touch
of dew on the skin long after the sun.

ii

He tells me how the novelist made maps in another life.
I tell him that the man is older now and sips tiny cups
of green tea as he stares through the misted panes
of his English cottage, the house smelling too much
of gas and boiling cabbage.

The librarian smiles, his wrinkles showing at last.
He leads me slowly along corridors, then unties the folders
to show me the neat, clean-edged surveyor's charts
of my friend the novelist. His lettering is even as always,

and the circular patterns of the earth's topography
are carefully mapped on the jaundiced sheets.
His notes read like a man reporting discovery for the first time,
with muted awe, yet dutiful to detail like a soldier.

His companions are all listed in the tidy ledger
of labourers, porters, cooks, guides, and poets
(like the drunk who fled from his wife, his daughter,
his nation, and a demon poem that turned septic on him
one too still night of hubris and rum, the man who talked
to his shadow and cursed his ear for the sounds it ate),
their wages, their debts, their rations their vanishings.

iii

It is harder, though, to chart the smell of a country,
the concentric mixing of the mud-washed
market with its brown earth-heavy scent
of vegetables bleeding; yams, like elephantine
fingers, white and seeping where the knife
cuts; the impotent regularity of lime green
okras; the glowing violet of obscene garden eggs.
How do you sketch the rotting scent of a mammal's
carcass dangling from rusty hooks, trying
to suck in the salt sea spray to preserve itself
from the crawl of maggots? How do you write
the city's stench, the gutters breeding mosquitoes
as huge as wasps, giddy drunk and brazen like flies?
This earth defies the cartographer's even lines,
the tidy predictability of shapes, the neat names with precise
capitals, no smudge, no uncertainty of the hand. It is hard to tell
that the land has shifted, blooming new contours.
The charts cannot change as fast as the ironic jungle.
We have come this way before, I am certain,

but the landmarks are not exactly what they were.
The river is now a bow, now a crescent where once
it was straight, or so it seemed. The natives ask no questions;
they sniff the air, move their eyes, and live.
The cartographer, I know, understands the fiction
of this telling, the lines are myths, dream-stories
in the faces of his crew. The only constant is the psychotic
lament of Wagner and a bloody warrior wail from the Warrau soldier
who has followed the scent of this march for weeks like a breeze.
The notes of music are caught in the foliage.
On the way back, they have only just began to drop
like shed leaves in the blackened creeks of this hinterland.

iv

Across the river's mouth, light circles still the slow water into glass
and a canoe silhouettes poetically; the body of its pilot
is a divining twig leaning towards the mawing delta.
Sometimes it seems a joke, this ordering of dreams, this flattening
of the history of the world, of the heart into a faded yellow chart.
And when we least expect it, the jungle bursts through
the thin parchment, splitting it to shreds, leaving us lost again.

The novelist is dying now, and with him a generation of dialects
to speak the earth, the mist, the light, the river. There is no language
on the water, all is cloudy. Soon the canoe is a mere smudge.

UMPIRE AT THE PORTRAIT GALLERY

At the Portrait Gallery near Trafalgar Square
I am searched by an ancient umpire
who mumbles his request with marbles or loose
dentures in his mouth. I see my first
portrait: the blotched bony fingers, the warts,
the clumsy overlarge gold ring loosely turning
like it will when he is entombed for good;
that look of boredom around the eyes
he masks with considered politeness
like a drunk man's careful compensations
and this self-important thinning of lips;
the nose, the greenish veins, the cliché
of a mole on his brow. It is too dark here
to study him well, besides he has found nothing
and the natives are restless at my back.

I am looking for the faces of this country;
the rustic, the jaundiced, the worn,
sharp tight snaps so close the pores talk;
faces caught in unaware blankness,
the rituals of rocking to numb silence
on the trains; dirty light, the thin
mist of darkness in the underground
making the faces collectors' bits,
keepables of a post-nuclear tribe.

I find only the posed stateliness
of another time – the courtly manners,
the clean colours staring from the palette
masking the stench and filth of older ways –
nothing to write about, really, nothing.

I am back in the lobby staring at the native,
his Adam's apple bobbing, his fingers,
the thick blackened nails, the stale suit,
the cap, the poem he is – the simple grammar
of another time – the years of the bombs
falling; he must have seen broken bodies
too. Now he fingers my underthings
searching for what I may have taken.
He finds nothing, nods me along.
Still, the globular ring keeps me
from forgetting him altogether,
that and the absence of stories to tell.
It is brilliant outside. A black-faced
Bobby points me the way to the Southern
Bank where the river reeks of history
and word weavers converge in snotty halls
to flaunt their musings to the world.
Here we are in the carcass of empire
searching in vain for sweetest honey.

BAPTISM

Kingston

i

In a corner of the city
where the seawater meets
the salvaged zinc
of basic shacks, with
their paint pans
packed with soil
she carried from Browns Town
(where everything is luxuriant
but two ends can't meet)
nurturing some cerasee
and mint leaf
trying to turn the beach
into a village
where everything black
even the sand;

you come to play campaigner
on a spirit-filled night
when the earth is rumbling
with the drum and the sub-
terranean journey of spirits
from out the sea bottom
and their heads are lashed
like flags of dignity;
then spinning, spinning
in impossible waves of skirts
white and billowing whiter.

That night at home
you chisel tame the rock
of our salvation in a rush
trying to catch the swirl
before it leaves your head,
trying to contain the knock
of your temple hurling blood
into your arms, your thighs
carving from some ancient
granite the stilled motion
of the dance, the fist
of power, the calm sleep
of wide-eyed possession
the arc of light taking shape
on the body of a believer
and carrier, a mounted
soul, turning, turning,
like it has been doing
since the ships set sail
from the Guinea coast.

South Carolina

In 1920 in South Carolina
Africans look like Africans.
They are standing in the river
the lush of swamp vines
thick beards of moss
misting them in soft light.

The girl in the middle with her toes
clutching the mud of the river bottom
is to be dipped back deep, deep
by pastor and deacon full of power
then to be pulled back up
raised above the earth,
wet but the better for it – Amen.

There is a song hanging in the air.
It is morning and a butterfly
turns and flits about
her bandannaed head.

MIDLAND

for Krystal

i

A Letter From Greeleyville

Dear Claudia,
Few things here succumb to time though the old grow tender
and die. Still, they appear again in the new light,
same face, same open skirts, same fingers clutching pipes
smoking a halo about their heads, rocking a blues on the same porches.
You would like this place for a time, but I know you will long
for the clean efficiency of your city — the stench of manufactured age.
The scent of jasmine and the dank earthiness of this soil
soaked by an old river, so long silted by the runoff
of a generation of fears, detritus, and funky bundles
of hair, sin, phlegm, blood passed out each month,
shoved, clumped, burnt into the blooming ground, remind me
of Sturge Town in St. Ann where my grandfather is buried
in a thick grotto of *aloe vera* and stunted pimiento trees.
But this place speaks a language I have to learn, and this woman
who travels with me introduces me to the earth and her folks
as a stranger, a specimen from far away. I pretend I do not feel
the welling of tears when I smell the old sweat of her grandmother's
housedress hanging from a nail on the back of an oak door.
The corn has turned a rotten gold and pale in the summer,
the twine of leaves and roots dark and spotted while the mildewed glory
of old hymnals seeps from the St. James Baptist church
where the blues have marinated the boards till they are supple
with the fluent pliability of faith so old it knows the ways of God
like it knows family, and blood ties. I am stealing things from here
and sending them to you, knowing you are too decent to use them.
But do, keep them safe till I arrive for a spell, and then I will find
good use for these sweet collectibles, lasting things. Love, Kwame.

226

Blues on Highway Fifteen with Krystal

At midmorning, we watch the green of tobacco stanzas,
such even reckoning of this state where a nation carved its name
into Cherokee country, making a new landscape, ploughs turning the earth
to the slow assured cadence of the Baptist hymns, the rebel yells,
the scalper's knife. Yet there is something tender here.

We are riding Highway Fifteen through Manning towards Kingstree,
searching for Alma's meditation on home in the sweetly pained
bourbon-grooved voice of Lady Day that Krystal plays
again and again, punching viciously at the knobs, rushing the tape
back to its beginning. And Lady Day conjures the skeletal twist of an oak
somewhere where the torture of fear and the faraway cry of the dead
are the same, despite the tundra cold. Krystal points to a green bluff,
a tree isolated against an indifferent blue sky – *Like that*, she says.
*The common trees, the quality of light in the sky. I sat under that tree
once – I don't remember why, but we sat there, me and my mother,
and we ate sandwiches, and she was crying for no good reason.*

iii
In Search of Alma

After the storm, the ravaging of the earth,
the stripping of green, the pounding of winds
on tender flesh; after the howling,
the green grows hungrily over everything,
and how quickly the multitude of sins
is covered by the crawling of wisteria and kudzu.
This earth speaks no memories of wrongs done;
there is a sweet politeness here, a way of decency,
the value of perfume in damp kerchiefs outside
the outhouse where the flies buzz rudely.

I have come to seek out Alma's lament,
to scratch into her grave, and find the rot,
of crumbling softness that was her paler self.

iv

Crow Over Corn Row

Above the shock of cotton trees hovers a solitary
bird, against the sky. It is black and stays only long enough
to seem like a portent. Standing in the cotton groves, I pluck
the coarse filthy white tangle from the grey brittle unlipping
of the flower. There is nothing like the hint of a vulva's softness here;
all juice dried out, the earth gives up its beaten self
in the language of simple cotton, the tight tangle
of the squat bushes, the debris from years of shedding
upturned like the unexpected shallow graves
of massacred millions. I pluck at the stubborn seeds
until the ball of cotton is softer in my palm.
The bird swoops, turns, and fades into the blue.
This short peace defies the rustle of old ghosts
quarrelling in the twisted ribbons of the corn leaves.
It is hard to breathe in this heat and stench; easier to drive on,
the wind cupped by the car, warm relief on a wet body.

v

Roosting

I drive towards the burnt-out Baptist church
with its well-kept graveyard – green, flowered –
and blackened walls desecrated with familiar
hatred, hieroglyphs of a twisted myth.

'*You have just received a courtesy call from the knights
of the Ku Klux Klan. Don't make the next be a business call.*'

228

I remember the bird, black as a crow
or raven chattering over the cacophony of corn,
uncertain of a place to land, so he moved on.

But the symbol is too convenient – too balanced.

Now a flock of audacious crows stare
into the gutted sanctuary, shaded by the fresh
whiteness of blooming dogwood.
They are roosting, as if they have found a place to haunt,
as if the feet of some long forgotten dead
were shod with shoes for walking by ignorant folks,
as if no one pointed their heads East to home.

I keep a piece of burnt timber as a souvenir,
my fingers growing black with the soot.
The silence prays over me.

vi

Decent Folk

A voice, high as a counter-tenor, shatters the eaves;
the aria of a storm twisting its path through
the thick peach groves of this blood-soaked land
high like a castrato gallivanting through
a Handel requiem, a lament for the dead;
this sound is bearded, broad-chested and cynical,
it is ripping through the state, now, seasoned
by the warmth of Florida's serrated coastline,
and the family gathers to whisper prayers as the world
crumbles around them. The blackness is heavy.
They pass down their stories to the wail of death
warding off the tears with the preserved narratives
of survival. What they speak are lies, the truths

229

are entombed secrets, the ritual secrets of rural folk,
still decent enough to know that talking about
love between that cracker Buddy Lawrence
and Powie, sweet Powie, is sacrilege, sinful,
plain indecent. No one thinks to ask how
twelve babies, yellow and pink, came howling
from that smoky womb. No one thinks to ask
how come he dies there in the house he built
for her, the wind blowing like it is now,
and the next generation staring at this man,
this white man breathing his last right under
the flared nostrils of Jimmy Crow. No one asks
nothing. Powie was raped, is all. The rest
is silence and the dignity of black folks
cultivated on this equivocal land, the rows
even, the time of harvest arriving like the moon,
relentless, the way it has always been, always will be.

vii

Epoch

> 'I moan this way 'cause he's dead,' she said.
> 'Then tell me, who is that laughing upstairs?'
> 'Them's my sons. They glad.'
>
> *Invisible Man* by Ralph Ellison

Krystal, an epoch glows beneath your skin.
Your nose spreads like flattened clay, your lips,
bloody grapefruit, wet, startled crimson.
You hurried your make-up, and the base is too pale
for your skin. You have no time for the paletting,
the mixing of hues to find the dialect of your history.
There is the epoch of silence in your skin,
something hidden, a curse in the long of your lower back
before the deviance of your buttocks.

230

A family of tangerine people; your folk are black,
thoroughly African, southern folk shaped in the kerosene-smelling
back quarters, where old pork was cured; at night, the flies, groggy,
drunk with the heat, and Buddy Lawrence panting into this soil,
this tendon tight woman, making babies with transparent skin.
Powie begat Alma begat Okla begat Lynne begat Krystal: the years
do not seem enough between the ash and tar of a Sumter lynching
and the promise of better days. Your skin does not trust its language
of appeasement. You stand in the stark sun, trying to darken your skin,
but it grows transparent in the heat, and all is palimpsest,
the language of blood underneath your skin.

viii

To the Third and Fourth Generations

You too carry the soup of nausea, the taste of a man's forced breath
behind you, the crawl of his hands cupping at your flesh,
the thought of dreaming your face into the wide spaces of the low
       country
where the bandy-legged, tobacco chewing cliché of a farmer came
       to find
the perfect lip and tongue of your ancestor. Still, at night,
you dream his head, too heavy for the smallness of his body,
his tiny hands open, trying to touch your nipple.
And you wish for an instant that he were the cracker, Buddy Lawrence,
so you could, for Powie, for Alma, for the host of mothers, leave
       him castrated
and bleeding in the half light. But his hair kinks, his eyes are black
as Elmina's dungeons, and his smile reeks of the disarming sweet of
       a Motown song.
You will not write this down. You will store it quietly, like Powie did,
trusting that the ruined cells will seed into another womb, another
       generation
free enough to interpret and speak the genetic vernacular of anger.

Somebody Trouble the Water

Wade in the water
Wade in the water, children
Wade in the water…

In a dream, I am in the Sahara with its tongue of heat
on the edges of Egypt. The sand is carnelian, stained with old
      sacrificial pots.
The shards are all that remain. It has been centuries and still,
in the early morning, a girl walks slowly, the soft sand slipping under
      her feet;
a smudge of white flutters in her hands rippled by the wind's lick.
On a perfectly smooth rock, she batters the tender dove,
its blood gleaming on the stone. She pulls out the soft viscera
and reads them while the new sun splatters the mountain's face.
She is a dream so distant she seems worth forgetting.
But she changes, as dreams tend to, and it is you, Krystal, who stands
      there,
over the grave of Alma, this time, your palms open, the wet tissue speckled
by the green above you. You have been crying, making, I can tell,
unreasonable covenants with the dead, with the living,
with the mountains at your back in this place of silence.
This South's sores are still too fresh. A hand plunged
into the earth will touch the sticky moisture of its brokenness.
You've got to sing those songs just to keep on keeping on, Krystal.

Wade in the water
Wade in the water, children
Wade in the water
God's gonna trouble the water
God's gonna trouble the water.

EASTER SUNDAY

'I was getting savage.'
Joseph Conrad

The nail clip unfolded, catches the light
like an origami insect of aluminium foil.
My nails, crudely clipped, gather in a pile
of opaque ivory on the gleaming porcelain,
waiting among the single pubic hair
like the paraphernalia of an obeah man
about to tie me for good. I can
stare at these meaningless objects
of my life, the evidence of flesh remaking
itself, the rituals of the civilised,
warding off the encroachment of the beast,
the barren heart of a callous ape.
I read *National Geographics* on the toilet
after midnight, to calm my dreams
now taking shape around the sound
Rosewood, the brute film of Florida's
lynching history; so familiar the cowardly
bravado of white men spewing *nigger*
like an aphrodisiac to their impotent selves.
I do not want to dream of blood tonight;
tomorrow is purple resurrection day, Christ's
ginal game, that genius disappearance.
I want to break unleavened bread
with my brother, son of the beast in the dark
grinning at the charred stump of a black man
turning in the kerosene haze of Rosewood.
I clip my nails, watch the projectile crescents
dart around the tile until I am man again,
trimmed to the clawless perfection of man.

Now, perhaps, I will dream of fossils,
the primordial sway of a Yanomami hammock,
and the bland narratives of alien people,
Von Humboldt's 'fierce people' guarding the portals
of the Orinoco's source. I transfer my dialect of ire
into myth; trying to beat back that lament
of a gospel song, blue and relentless as truth,
unfolding the apostrophe of the hung man dangling
from a live oak like the worm's silk cocoon.

NEW POEMS

FAT MAN

How terrible the confession, *We are all dying.*
The way fat weighs us and the heart swells
from too long labouring to make us breathe, slouch
and snore with guttural dreadfulness (the terror
of it). I do not want to die. So absurd
this admission, this effort to confront
the unpredictable odds of our living. But fat
people die quickly – we know this – and I,
too, too solid with the mess of casualness
grow fat with age. So hard to come back.
I stare at my stranger self in hotel mirrors.
I am afraid to meet this stomach-glorious
creature, unable these days to find an angle
of satisfying grace. I am now a circle of errors,
the fat has taken over. Perhaps pride in this
plump existentialism will make it well,
but my child seems too, too small, helplessly
small in my clumsy cumbersome arms.
They, my children, will call me fat,
and I will resent their kindnesses
and compensations for my limp and waddle.
I dream of sweat, the familiar
hint of muscles beneath the inner flesh,
the rib, a reminder of the body
so vulnerable beneath this cloak of flesh.
I dream of breathing easily when I bend
in two to touch my shoelaces. I dream
of better days when I will leap lightly,
a slender man gambolling in the mirror's face.

THE OLD MAN

For CL and CC

I found myself yesterday; my old self,
the self I thought I had lost to memory,
the self I hope for when I ask old friends,
people who knew me then, *Tell me
what I was, who I was, twenty years ago,
when my zeal, missionary and so intact in faith,
was what went before me?* They usually
say there is nothing different in me, just more
flesh, more beard and little new – but I know
they lie. They too have forgotten – or perhaps
they prefer the jolly, flawed, slightly decayed
me, the fleshmonger, the fat one with no spartan
instinct. I am so accommodating now of the dirt
in the mix (I read Rushdie the apostate with shocking
comfort). But yesterday on one of the narrow
streets in the centre of Basseterre, the algae-green
slimy gutters reminding us of how humans live
chucked up in villages that spread into each other,
somewhere in the half-light of a Chinese restaurant
with its reeking toilet and a large wooden crate
full of chicken fat and a plague of drunk flies
kotched at the landing above the flight of raw
cement stairs, we ate a meal, succulent
despite the squalor, and she told me
that she did not know the me she is meeting now.
I was, she recalled, through the gauzy memory
of three neat rums, a straight man, a righteous man,
an arrow. She shaped her hands into an axe, slashing
the air. A serious man, an unsmiling, frowning man
who made plays so full of the shed blood of salvation;
plays that bludgeoned the hapless audience with faith,
while the prayer team's bursts of tongues and song

seeped through from backstage into the house.
And the me, the round, jocular me she met here
in this crude miniature island, is not the man
I was. I feel the weight of my liberty, a stone
about my legs. Her love, her respect, her care
not to offend could not overcome the ribaldry
of the rum, and she stared at me telling me the joke
of the radio host whose fellating lover began
to send *Greetings to Puncie in Hermitage.*
She watched me to see what I will do, hoping
it is clear, that I would curse the wiles of Satan.
I laughed, insisting that I could be tarnished.
This too rotten core, the memory of me
I had forgotten embarrassed me, scowled
at me. She brimmed with tears as she looked at me:
not joy, but such sadness at the ending
of all reliable things, the end of faith, the end
of conviction, the dismantling of old expectations.

MEETING

It rains. The blistered skin of this city
  cools. Summer has been an endless circle
of labours — the heat, the rituals of our lives.
  At noon, the rain stammers to a drizzle,

and the thin glow of light catches the bodies
  of women moving quickly; black women
bent low, hurrying through the damp cool.
  I watch a body, the promise of a smile

in the round of her hips, the rapid nervous
  pace of her, and I take her in as one does
with a familiar moment — a vaguely comforting
  pattern. This has happened before,

a moment with a stranger, imagining
  that she too will turn and grin — I think
of the delicate ribbons of a woman's
  laughter as she comes closer. On the edge
of sin, the naked welcome, I see it is you

and I feel like a strange man waiting to touch
  you with words. In this indiscretion
I want to say I fear losing you; I am
  angry at me for being that strange man

taking you in as a predator does. Your smile
  disarms me, its trust and pleasure in our
accidental meeting — and the rain gathers
  again in the sky. You hand me the car keys.

We say something about money and time,
  and you hurry away, your hips — my hips,
the bloody world's hips — swinging sweetly
  while I cradle in me the terrible fear of love.

BRISTOL

I leave the cold wet of Bristol. A city of dull
spires and the ostentatious slave money
of the *nouveau riche* who built grand estates
and created a stained empire. The city
is changing. Old hints of glory are relics
and the water in the gorge crawls brown,
its concrete lips darkened by rain,
cracked in long fissures. Above is the Clifton
Bridge – that useless act of genius: Egyptian
anchors, towers on two sides, the gorge
below. The marvel of it, the absolute
hubris of it! This slave money makes you
think of empire in all things: Ah grandeur!

I limp along the country lanes. The fat
has been falling away each day. Stress
and the sorrow of a life shattered all eat
at the sullied flesh. My calf is strained
by cold and weight. I have lived in a red
call box, making petitions across the Atlantic
each morning before light; an onlooker
would call it love though it feels like pain
here in Bristol on these long gloomy days.

How easy it is to find nothing of poetry
in a week of patterns: the hills, the castles,
the mansions, the bums, the drunken
students, the moribund theatre, the bland
food, such dull simplicity. I leave quietly
at dawn, mutter polite farewells
to the inquisitive landlady who stands
there smiling as if on the verge of thought,
but so nervous, waiting to be mugged or hugged.

I say goodbye to her cheapness,
and think of the furnace I have kept
burning day after night despite the rules;
the dingy room a sauna – her sheets soaked
in my sweat, and smelling of my tears,
from long nights haunted by dead slaves,
their unsettled shadows drifting
across the Clifton Bridge.

November is a clumsy month in this iambic
amble towards the dysfunction of Christmas.
Jean, brilliant and full of outrageous wit,
is consuming bottles of red wine. Her stories
leap with the clarity of revelations in the room
thick with sensimilla — a flower in a dung heap.
The sun blazes late in the afternoon
through the thin fingers of naked trees,
something like a finale before the gloom.
The mulch of leaves in the mud and filth
of the streets smell of London, again.
Again, I am leaving London and this dinner
is not for me though it feels like it is.
The table has the strained effort
of Jamaican nostalgia — fried plaintains,
curry goat, escovitch fish — all blandly
flavoured, as all reproductions
must be. We all speak loudly in patois as if
we have rediscovered a mother tongue.
It has been too many years since
immigrant garnered in us the loyalty
of survivors. Now we ritualize our
storytelling into something quite dead
here in November with the asthmatic
buses, the congested lanes, the mute
masks of the underground labourers.
Kiss, kiss, turn the other cheek, air
embrace. *May you endure the winter*
well, friend, and do remember to cover
the deep scar in the back garden where
the old flowering tree keeled over
and died of some consumptive disease.
Keep warm and I will send you pressed

sorrel petals from the Clarendon hills…
Such good wine, where you get it?
So dry and yet oddly wet…I must be
drunk… We laugh delicately, hopefully,
and watch our love, the genius poetess,
gazing dumbly at the disquiet of the blunt
season of Yule, muttering, *I can feel it*
a-come on, the euphoria, the flight,
the leap outwards stretching, dear saviour,
for solace… So we lay hands on her tender head,
tangle our prayers in her unruly locks,
and imagine healing as pure as memory – *Bright eye,*
Bright eye, mek yuh eye dem wet soh?

BIRTHRIGHT

The narrative is a myth, not history, not in the blood:
the cricket, the books, the poems, the stories,
the lovers, (such unfaithfulness), the instinctive
charm, long letters, the tongue of seduction
all of these as if the blood carries sin
from generation to generation. But it is all myth,
an inheritance stolen one careless night
in Mandeville. A man dying. A son caught
in the slow moving air. A mother hymning
this deathwatch. It is as if something
is being passed. The thing is, I was there,
and no one else made it, and I took what I could
in that hour of lamentation. There in that night,
the green city so dark it turned everything
into a deep moving space, I looked again
at that photo and accepted the imputed glory.

Now, nearly twenty years later, I return to that photo
of two men walking along the Thames,
somewhere near a chapel, the BBC behind them,
its dark cold studios where in that hour
at the microphone they smelt the humid
saltiness of their island. For that quiet hour
they deposited love in the cadence of their native
talk. Then it turned into painful nostalgia
and longing in the sudden blast of the air off the river,
the stench of history and dog shit on the long street
beside the ornate chapel (grey and stolid against a pewter
sky); beside the statue of horses with bursting muscles
and grimaces; beside this place spared by the Luftwaffe;
the geriatric empire whose doddering they called
a well-kept swagger (they were still believers).

The two men are walking towards the camera
with the wind flapping their baggy trousers
around their thin legs. On the left is our father —
so odd that he is younger than I am now,
so odd the way I want to mistake him
for me. But sandals, worn corduroys
and the dust and bush landscape were my youth,
and besides, he is thin (*these minor famines*,
says Swanzy, the kind BBC chap), which makes him
fit-looking. Hunger is a constant condition,
the uniform of the desperate artist like the narrow tie,
the billowing slacks, the tweed jacket
with leather elbow patches, the empty pipe.
His eyes, his scraggly beard, his bright gaze
are thirsty for a pint and carefree laughter.

ii

I see you, Mastermind, and not me in him. He was
twenty-five and could still not boast a convincing
beard, and you, at thirty, are still cultivating,
shaving and then watching to see if it will
come to full chin-cover. Your hair, too, is receding,
the strong thin legs, the look, bright with longing —
all you, not me as I have always wanted to imagine.
You wash-bellies, you are constantly assured
of your genius, yet never certain of when it will
be fulfilled. But mothers always believe; mothers —
yours and his — always hold that faith deep in them.

iii

This is *your* heritage. I have stolen
much, first the photo, and then the idea
of the photo, as if that was me by the Thames.
But what is fe yuh cyaan un-fe-yuh.

246

I am the counterfeit inheritor, fortunate
to have beeen at the right place when these things
were given out. Ask Jacob. It was never
diabolic and he, like me, had God to blame.
But I am the wrong corpus for the melancholic
blue notes of a heart so broken, so hidden –
the language you understand so well.

And this was his vernacular, the complex
in those eyes, beady and bright against the grey
of London. Me, I am the caretaker, the keeper
of secrets, the one who borrowed his wisdom
and art and wore it well. These things I have taken
as if they were mine. I can't be blamed.
Even *he* thought me the heir; even *he* longed
to make me the next chapter. We arranged it,
the cricket, the school, the English Literature,
the big talk of Oxford because we all believed.

But tipsy with your insanities, you have known
it all along, though for years stayed silent
until that dark shed with the lizards
and the haunting broke something in you.
It is the way of narratives of blood
that are untidily ribboned in old myths.
It is the way of stolen birthrights, the messy
contracts we make with blood legacies.

VERNACULAR

for Paul Monette

On a sunset beach at summer's end, a man
balances the judgement of the world on the tips
of his outstretched hands: a flirtation
with the language of damnation and salvation.
A lover enacts a myth – an old narrative that love,
too, in the face of gaunt death, is possible –
how trite, how Paul McCartney, all that fluff.
T.V. tragedy is reliable for its arcs, its tears,
its climaxes at quarter to, and its tidy denouements.
So I make stanzas of a man dying of AIDS,
his lover buoyant, the golden hour at hand,
and I write of you, of brothers who love.

Two brothers tumble like lovers.
They are in their parents' marriage bed
where all mystery was discarded so long
ago and what is left is the security
of entwined smells, the smells of love –
a woman's intimate muskiness and flowers,
a man's old sweat and clean vodka cool.
They are too young to know the taboo, too caught up
in the riot of their blood to translate the idioms
of eroticism. What is left is the memory
of bonds, like the secret of how we grew
to rely on the smell of sweat in our clothes.
I can tell he is my brother by his smell.
This is the tale of our redemption.
We are grown men, now. Fathers,
we have planted our seed, written poems,
made love, held the body of an aging parent,
whispered secrets, tumbled back
into a scattering of tongues, dry leaves stirring.

The memory is as fine as the day
it happened in the green filtered light
of Neville's and Mama's room; the coolest
room with windows crowded by crotons
and hibiscuses garlanded by giddy
hummingbirds. That room of comforts:
Old Spice, make-up talc, and Noxema.
Neville is dead now, and I don't shave
so I have no use for the off-white flasks
of Old Spice. We do die. It is the way
of the world, it is how myths are made.

A man on t.v. turns in the sand – a gay white man
I would never know or like, but his poem
carries to me quietly, a universe in words,
a vernacular I understand as mine, the dialect
of two men loving, not lovers, but brothers,
crossing time with memory and haunting.

IMPOSSIBLE FLYING

Palms of victory/ Deliverance is near!
1980 JLP Election Song

i

On Kingston's flat worn earth,
everything is hard as glass.
The sun smashes into the city – no breath,
no wind, just the engulfing, asthmatic noonday.

We move with the slow preservation
of people saving their strength
for a harsher time. 1980:
this land has bled – so many betrayals –
and the indiscriminate blooding of hope
has left us quivering, pale,
void, the collapsed possibilities
causing us to limp. We are a country
on the edge of the manic euphoria
of a new decade: Reagan's nodding
grin ripples across the basin's
surface. We dare to dream
that in the spin and tongues of Kapo
perhaps we too will fly this time,
will lift ourselves from the slough
of that dream-maker's decade –
the '70s when we learned things we only
suspected of ourselves: our capacity for blood,
our ability to walk through a shattered
city, picking our routine way to work
each morning. We are so used now to the ruins,
perhaps more than that, perhaps to wearing
our sackcloth and ash as signs of our
hope, the vanity of survival.

In that decade when a locksman
could prance the streets with a silver
magic trail in his wake, how we fought
to be poor, to be sufferers, to say
Looking at you, the better one—how
we cultivated our burden-bearing,
white squall, hungry belly,
burlap-wearing, Cariba-suited
socialist dream. And reggae
with its staple of faith, fame
and fortune spoke its revolution
from the speakers of souped-up
BMWs. Gone now, all gone.

We have thrown off that dead skin now.
And the fleets of squat Ladas
are rusting, O Havana.
We've grown too cynical for such austerity
or perhaps we did not suffer enough.
So on such blank startled days, we dream
of flight. How we hope: *Dance!*
Dance, damn it! Dance, damn it! Be happy!
Our apocalypse echoes on the sound system
and we dance. These laws, these new laws,
these palm leaves, these clamouring bells,
so desperate for deliverance,
this insipid green in the future, and we all
stare at the unflinching sky
and will our hearts to fly.

ii

And how you ran, sprinting
down Carlisle Avenue,
your face set against the bare wind.

You were making, your arms spread
undulating in complete faith
in the wind's lift,

the physics of the updraft.
Past the low fences,
the skittish yelping dogs,

the streaks of telephone wires,
the hibiscus hedges;
a blur of green and pink

and smudged off-white.
And me calling you,
trying hard to bring you back.

Me catching up,
behind you now, our heat,
our panting, the slap of bare feet

on the soft asphalt.
And I reached for you
held you by the waist,

drawing you down,
and it felt in that instant
not like a shattering of faith

but a struggle to keep
you home, for each tendon
of your body throbbed

with the lightness of a body
prepared for flight.
And my betrayal was to become

the burden,
the anchor you had
for years longed to shake off.

The stillness, the gaping crowd
staring at this sudden accident –
two men in a heap

of twisted limbs
on the road;
you saying, *This time, this time,*

this time if you had let me,
it would have happened,
I too felt the vanity

of our beaching.
The bells shimmered –
the dispatches were in:

No one
was flying
no more.

PRE-MORTEM

For Neville

i

I have tried to recall this as one would seasons,
but the island is a monotone of sun and occasional
rain, rapid and consuming – everything softening
before the hard light of an eleven o'clock sun.
It may have been April – for the poetry of it. I pluck
it, dangle it, adorn it with the Easter sermons
of spilt blood seeping from the A.M. radio.
In Kingston, after the clutter of traffic dies
down, after I turn into the tree-thick Avenue
off Barbican Road, late at night, the street
a black disquiet stretching into the hills,
the sound of an old transistor carries like sound
under water. The sharp orange spot
of light moves in slow arches. A ritual
as comforting as meditation is being enacted.
The scent of Rothmans meets me – it is as if
I am in another place, high in the St. Ann Hills,
Sturge Town, your town where you tasted
first fruit, where the voices of old once-
slaves moved through the black nights
repeating the secrets of duppies, long-tongued,
sweet-toothed phantoms that sipped the drip
of molasses easing its smooth way through
the cured wooden barrels knocking against
the soggy deck of the rocking cart. Hear 'im,
If de molasses so sweet, how tas'e de sugar?
I find you on the verandah, B.T. Williams
grinding at his sermons, and my brother,
your son, sits beside you. Together,
you listen to these sermons as if you have come

to church to find in this forgiving darkness
grace, salvation, peace and forgiveness
for those years of faithlessness, the pragmatic
suspension of belief in the Marxist dream.

ii

The power has been gone for hours, the candles
have melted to hard puddles in the Milo
tin covers, and I sense that you two –
old man and boy, once strangers and now
friends, equals, co-conspirators in the dark –
are plotting how to share the acts of care Mama
offers. She is mothering both of you now.
The chemicals have slowed the younger,
and despair in this new season
of unemployment, dreams souring
and the absence of poems, letters and stories
have halted the elder. I imagine now, jealously,
what secrets you are sharing, what stories,
what lies, what silences, what tears.
I do not stay with you. I can not.
Instead, I walk into the pause, then,
stumbling into the humid house,
I hear the rush of whispers and chuckles
fill the vacuum of my wake. I know
that in this I have found the mystery of his calm
acceptance when you died those months
later, in another season, on another familiar night.

RESURRECTION
Kingston, 1980

After the year of cataclysm, the walls of this city
are scarred with green and orange hieroglyphs of hate,
the tragic lies of false prophets; the rubble,
the stones, the air still thick with last breaths –
800 blasted lives – and palms and bells, rods
and anthems strewn around, the detritus
of a celebration we won't ever understand.
We have bled out our peace. Those nights
we trembled, remember? The righteous
and the fallen have fled. The city
is dusty, broken after years of neglect.
How we suffered for a dream, recycled
our glad rags into simpler things –
such sacrifices we made in that valiant,
austere decade. The season of cataclysm
still haunts our city, and we dance
our spastic Restoration, a world of vain
hope: the coke, the untrammelled
sex, and in this world shadows
reach across our secret pleasures,
the last hours of healing. So little to love.
I travel this city with a stone for a tongue,
watching the light of a new moon.
I travel this road, with the limp of a survivor.
Sometimes the backfire of a car leaves me
washed with fear, my heart and head pulsing.
I walk into the gate of my *alma mater* –
once my sanctuary from the city – now alien.
It has been a year and everything seems
so trite, so malformed and rough hewn.
I pass through the rusting gates
framed by the languorous ficus berry trees;

the sound of an old doomsday hymn,
the schoolboy contraltos lamenting
in my head.
          Dear Jesus, this place smells
of revival and death. I come through the gate
with faith – tomorrow it shall be tested.
Holy Spirit, breathe on me, breathe on me!
It is six and dusk; Simms Building is alabaster
in the gloom. This silver deadness
is the sepulchre of the unrisen dead. I see you,
Mastermind, leaning against the tongueless
bell, your eyes emptied of all reason.

WARD TWENTY-ONE

The dirt track turns to marl in the wind tunnel
between Maternity – the pale yellow gowns of swollen
women a constant slash of light through the grey
louvres – and the whitewashed ward where you are.
My heart grows as I walk by casually,
trying to pretend I have forgotten your eyes pleading
with me in the brightly lit greeting room;
you pointing to the stumble and glossolalia
of the pretty girl who does not care that her breasts
are poking through the too small hospital issue
green tunic. Around us, the sterile slow pace
of madness medicated. Like you I imagine
that you don't belong; I imagine you are too
astute, too collected for this; your pathologies
are civil things. Yet I see the scars
on your knuckles, and you drool; how you drool,
your tongue, not yours, just a clumsy lump
of meat in your mouth. You are telling me you need
to go, lucid as anyone I know, until you laugh,
reminding me of the morning I held you down,
tied your wings, did not have the faith;
and in that same clean logic, your eyes
stare steady at me as you speak in soft
conspiracy, *I would be flying now,*
you know that? I would be flying if you never
hold me down… It has been a week
since I stopped. That last time the orderlies
told me of the straps you strained against,
the electricity, the padded walls, the tears,
as if you were someone else, as if they needed me
to understand the lunatic's dialect, as if
they saw in me the hubris of class, or the hope
of sanity; as if I did not understand

the ordinariness of tragedy. That day I did not stop.
I simply bowed my head and walked away,
weeping; angry at my tears, at the
noble sorrow — as if it was me caught
in this wrestle with the chemistry
of the head — the demon tyranny.
I wept like an actor, testing each mood, swept,
yes, by the passion of the narrative,
but consumed by the tragic consequence
of fear. I wept as I walked the stony path
to Papine, helpless like that. Tonight
is the seventh night I have walked past.
It becomes easier, now. I fear only
that you will see me going by, not stopping.
Maybe you will see my lips moving, praying
for the miracle promised — another vanity —
the scripted prophecy of my peace.

CASTING OUT DEMONS

From the cave, a laugh gurgles, surfaces.
You have learned the dialect of my prayers,
a lingo of rules. You laugh, I cast it out;
they are legion; they keep returning. I imagine
your cave, the walls undulating with shadows.
I came to see you in the daytime, for despite
my faith, I fear the terror of night, the way
sudden light plays on my nerves. I imagine your
valley: the gloom, you wondering about
tomorrow's impossible equations. A week
ago, I dragged you from the toilet. I thought
I would find you bleeding. You were only
crying. I reached out. You held me, crushing me.

We trained you well. A ball smashed
over the fence and you always were our
emissary, the one to plead. You went
to test the waters, ask the old man
for the hard things, face wrath, face a gloom
we feared and the harshness of denial
with the genius art of tears and the open-
faced plea of the always infant.
They never said no. You think it nothing
now to walk through this, as if
in no time, you will come back grinning
rewarded with the ball in hand, answer ready.

I pray over your sharp forehead.
Your arms are sinew lined; you are
a thinner version of me and not strange enough
for the necessary detachment of strangers.
It is easier to cast out demons
from strangers because I am unfamiliar

with the line between personalities,
and my faith is not tested by the logic
of psychology. It is all spirit and fire.

I mutter my tongues; they turn like the thick
stale air in the room. I am waiting for them
to catch aflame, grow wings, make
your head light, clean, to return you to the boy
who used to laugh with me for hours
over a single image of Roman foot soldiers,
swatted by Asterix and Obelix, their sandals
suspended like an emptied coil of leather – the look
of comic violence. How we laughed.

The boy is gone. I want to find him,
but you are growing too quickly for him.
To return would be to retard all – the beard,
the voice, the dropping of fat, the age
in your eyes. Sometimes I see the fear,
as if so far in the recess of your cave,
you are trying to say something,
trying to grant me the faith to believe.

YELLOW

A deep pink face webbed in canary yellow netting,
swaddled in infant finery, flesh soft to the eye.
This is how we first met; you, unblinking,
a week old, and the order of my life shifted.
I was four and you seemed outside of me,
outside of meaning. The nine months before
were blank, no recollection of waiting
for what must have been our mother's
marvelously round alien body. For it to turn
to this.

      At four, I stared at the full-length
mirror, then sprinted to the back of it
to find my revenant. My first inexplicable
equation: the hide and seek of my image.
How easily it slipped away. At four,
all was accommodation of mysteries: a new baby,
the advent of snails after rain, the wide
valley of guinea-pig grass – a green, fluent sea
on which our cement and glass house sailed;
the magic appearance and disappearance
of this man, Neville, our father, who grinned
while bearing you as he did gifts
from exotic ports; smiling proudly
with that familiar gap-tooth and those
mischievous eyes grey as a blind man's
marble eye; bearing you, his lump of pink flesh,
eyes tightly shut, fingers curled.
Now the world had changed as worlds must.
Your coming was yellow like the blooming
of those poisonous bulbs flaming in the yard.

CHOKOTA

I pluck at memory to find the clues of you.
All is glitter and clean, white cement spotted by buffed
pebbles; metal, glass, porcelain, the tiles, this sixties modernity,
the louvres of green glass causing the unwavering blue light
to pattern the floor with a cool underwater mosaic,
the trees, the marl driveway, the rough cement walls, dusted
with a plague of gold, like pollen or something less wholesome.

Somewhere in this light, the hall empties, the guests have departed,
some lingering in the driveway, laughing, warm with spirits;
and you came to mimic the gestures of adults; moving from table
to table, from coaster to coaster, sipping the icy dregs left
for the gods – the good whiskey, gin, cognac, *akpeteshi*,
the metallic edge of such sweet aromas. You drank
until you collapsed where we found you, in the middle
of tables and chairs, drunk as a lord, so vocally drunk
you spoke like an Ashanti chief, as if somewhere
you had met one, poured libation with one, chewed
kola nut with one – laughing, slapping your thighs:
Bring me my chokota! It is amazing how prodigious
you seemed, bolstered by the liquor; how humble
we were staring at your man's way. We wanted to serve.

The panic, the sudden fear of not knowing you,
the tightening of my stomach, Mama's guilt-ridden
energy, Neville's bemused uncertainty, his arms dangling,
all seem too familiar now; the first rituals, really,
of your transformations. I suppose God does
prepare us sometimes with these comic *types*
for a larger tragic consequence, and we are better for it.

On his island where the myth of incredible
heroism from the squalor of a mundane life
is not a part of our dialect, our geniuses
walk ordinary paths through a people
that does not cheer, hoot, adore. The fall
is uneventful here, while in that other country
where the dream is a tenet of faith, your
cloistered devotion to making songs
would have been the natural discourse.
On the island you imagined
yourself juke-jointing in Memphis
twisting your body around a microphone,
with a swell of bodies reaching for you.
You filled page after page with the simple
hooks of pop songs – tunes we had no language
to describe or embrace. We had no language,
no head to see in you something that could leap
from the common into the remarkable.
We were hardly the dreamers, maverick
adventurers and quixotic clowns given to
reminding a nation that magic happens,
even here in these monotonous tropics.
Our sin was not mere benign indifference,
it was worse, it was unbelief, the tragic
foolishness of doubt, and we tried to show
you reality, to say that none of us,
ordinary, reasonable people, so grounded
in irony and an acute affliction of truth,
could be superstars. Our labours
to make our convictions truth in you
must have been enough to shatter
your mind and worse, your heart.

SECRETS

So young you learned the entrapment of secrets.
Your history is scattered across the city;
even strangers have seen you stumble, your heart beat
echoing in your head. They have shown pity
and collected your story; given you food
like alms for the poor. You dignify their pity.
On better days you walk the roads naked;
everyone knows you, knows of you. How easily
you laugh, not stalked by the fear of being revealed.
Who can hold threats over you? *Splashing good!*
you say, laughing, *Splashing good!* You let
it all hang out there. No mystery of your blood
is buried, no sin, no failing, no cheating,
no indiscretion, no embarrassment. It is all
out there, the life without secrets, a superstar's
life. So young, you have learned the tyranny
of discretion, learned to shun it — a simple lesson
I have learned only too late and with pain.
I have lived all turned in on myself, like a poem
trying to see the grace of a mountain's face,
but only caught up in the twisted entanglement
of roots imprisoned in the clay of myth,
my decency, my sanity, the lie of my life.
I am wracked now with the purest envy
for you whose liberty flits windily about you.

YOUR HANDS
for Mama

A mother cradles her child even when the head
grows too cumbersome for embrace, and for you,
who remain constant through these years,
it is hard to make poems since I come
always as a heavy head longing to be soothed.
It is mother love, I have learned: the tenderness
of your firm sculptor's palms greasy with Vicks
on my skin, the gentle intrusion of your fingers
searching my bowels for maddening worms;
the quick brush of your massage slick with pink
lotion, cooling the itchy cracked sores of the pox;
the calming voice, never panicked even when
I walked in at two in the morning, my body
splotched with welts the size of an open palm
from eating too many crab cakes (*If it has
not killed you yet, it won't – go to sleep*).
Still, after years, after imagining that I have
deserved your grace for my good son ways,
it is clear to me now that you always knew me
for the fragile child I was, the careful manager
of my pathologies, the marathon masturbator,
the author of clandestine lewd letters to lovers;
the boy afraid of the dark and of failure;
and yet you have loved. What you have
loved has never changed: my infant self,
my heart, my navel string, the umbilicus that ties me
to you, to home, to Ghana, to the instant
when the impossible pain of childbirth
propelled me out. This love was built
on the sacramental truth of those years.
Your hands molded my flesh, understanding
the pressure of skin on skin. How you love

is as simple as rainfall and dew at dawn.
My arrogance has been my millstone, and until
tonight's stumbling into tears and the hunger
for forgiveness and love, despite my
grievous sin, my flawed, uncertain self,
I never grasped the healing of your clay-
white hands, the familiar intimacy of your touch.

INDEX OF FIRST LINES

EXTRACTS FROM REVIEWS OF INDIVIDUAL COLLECTIONS

Progeny of Air

The book extends across a wide range of experiences, its first section focusing on incidents from childhood and adolescence. Many of these poems convey the painful cruelty of children, the pecking order of threat and coercion, terrible rites of passage. The playwright's skills of strong characterization are evident in the 'Hall of Fame', a series of vignettes of various characters, pupils and masters. The teachers are portrayed as figures of power and influence, but Dawes is aware of their off-duty lives too, striving to paint the whole picture. These portraits are invigorating and compassionate, suggesting that these men had futures as well as pasts, just like the boys on the threshold of adulthood. This is only one example of the way Dawes often offers a very different perspective on quite ordinary things, implying that time is more than simply a chronological device, and that culture and society is more than the hierarchy imposed upon 'the disorder of our terrible existence'. ... Dawes revels in the 'freedom to write the hidden.'

He takes many admirable risks, borrowing narrative techniques from the story-telling tradition and rhythms from reggae. His vocabulary is a curious mixture of formal precise or prosaic words together with street slang and surprising compounds, all informed by a love of traditional 'English' poetry instilled at school in Jamaica - 'the jazz of words against words / making beauty in rhythm, sound, in twisted / clash of constructs we did not really grasp // but felt...'

I am grateful to Kwame Dawes for writing this book and bringing some heat to a grey and chilly autumn; grateful also to the Forward panel of judges for awarding it their First Collection Prize and so bringing it to the attention of a wider audience. Peepal Tree are bringing out two further books. I look forward to seeing what else this man can do.

Linda France *Poetry Review*

Prophets

Dawes fuses charisma and comment, imagination and documentary, invoking elements from the genre of popular culture, sub-culture, Jamaican ethos and song, effectively and lyrically. The aspects of lyricism and song are crucial to the carriage of the book's narrative. Song works in multiple ways – as praise, as penance, as pursuant of peace, as provider of pleasure. Song is also rhythm, and rhythm is reggae - indigenous, pure, full of bass resonance - which quietly provides not only a chorus leit-motif but also the syllabic markers that anchor the overall scale and story. Clarice and Thalbot who play the role of the protagonists of this arching operatic tale are dextrously cast.

Kwame Dawes' may elicit comparisons with 'novels-in-verse' or 'poems-as-narrative novel', especially with works such as Vikram Seth's *The Golden Gate*, Derek Walcott's *Omeros*, Craig Raine's *History: The Home Movie*, or even King James' version of The Bible. If comparisons have to be made, they ought to be done setting one thing absolutely clear, that here is one writer who writes out of his own tissue, with intelligence, originality, and passion, employing his very own idiom. If there are influences, then the most likely tints of the spectrum would include Walcott, Bob Marley, Christianity, colonialism, but all of these obliquely and indirectly. *Prophets* is a major book, a feast of spontaneity set in a serious framework. It is a narrative poem of sheer power, contemporaneity, and hope; one that is full of beauty, sadness, wisdom, and true humanism.

Sudeep Sen

Requiem

Kwame Dawes' *Requiem* and *Jacko Jacobus* reveal a fresh talent, ready to take his place as one of the finest poets who has emerged during the 1990's. Like his two great compatriots, Derek Walcott and Kamau Braithwaite who, undoubtedly, represent the best tradition of Caribbean poetry, Dawes is similarly committed to capturing the essence of the Caribbean islands in expressions of compelling lyricism.

In *Requiem*, a work whose inspiration is derived from the illustrations of American artist, Tom Feeling's award-winning work, The

Middle Passage: White Ships/Black Cargo, Dawes relies on the lyric form of the elegy to re-create the the pain of suffering of slavery, and the possibility of redemption.

Indeed, in 'Requiem', the title poem, a lament for the many casualties of transatlantic slavery on the one hand and a celebration of hope on the other, the poet-persona reveals that he hears 'a blue note/of lament, sweet requiem/for the countless dead,/ skanking feet among shell,/coral, rainbow adze,/webbed feet, making as if/to lift, soar, fly into new days'. In 'Vultures', the poet finds an apt metaphor for the beneficiaries - in the purely commercial sense - of the inhuman crime of slavery: 'These vultures speckle a blue sky/and learn the trade routes/to the castles by the sea...' The gloom conveyed to the reader by the threnodic import of Dawes' imagery is remarkably tempered by a sense of hope, life, of survival, freedom: 'We sing laments so old, so true/then straighten our backs again.'

The technical accomplishment of Kwame Dawes' poetry is indicative of his ability to maintain a cool air while employing the genre of the lyric to explore his themes, and to cultivate an economy of expression while striving to maintain high quality in deployment of imagery.

Idowu Omoyele

Jacko Jacobus

The Caribbean is finding a big new voice of alarm in Kwame Dawes. Jacko Jacobus is a long rollickingly control biographical-political-erotical epic – a novel in two-line verse-form almost – but always a poem – inspire by that most socially intriguing of Old Testament Bible 'prophets', the story of Jacob & Esau

Already I hear this on radio, on CD, see it in flim & video

Where nex to, Jacko

Kamau Brathwaite

Shook Foil

Few poets capture the mood of a generation. In Shook Foil, Kwame Dawes, 'drawing on inspiration as diverse as Derek Walcott, T. S. Eliot and Lorna Goodison,' attempts to define reggae and the major personality behind the success of the music, Bob Marley. That Dawes chose Marley as the primary subject to explore the dimensions of reggae is no coincidence, for it was Marley who taught my generation how to be Jamaican and Pan-African (as if the two terms were mutually exclusive), how to honor ourselves and others, and finally how to love.

Throughout the collection, Dawes captures the many dimensions of reggae from the psalmic to the prophetic that are yet to be explored by other writers and musicians. Reggae remains unparalleled in its ability to absorb other influences and remain true to itself and to capture beauty, pain, and pleasure in a one-drop riddim. Its syncopation suggests a break, a gap – somewhere to fall with the faith that you will be caught - and this is what gives reggae its redemptive value. To really enjoy the music, you must believe. The same could be said of *Shook Foil*

Geoffrey Philp *The Caribbean Writer*

Midland

'A powerful testament of the complexity, pain, and enrichment of inheritance... It is a compelling meditation on what is given and taken away in the acts of generation and influence... There are different places throughout the book. They come willfully in and out of the poems: Jamaica. London. Africa. America. But all the places become one place in the central theme and undersong here: which is displacement... The achievement of this book is a beautifully crafted voice which follows the painful and vivid theme of homelessness in and out of the mysteries of loss and belonging.'

Eavan Boland